SOURCES OF CIVILIZATION IN THE WEST

Robert Lee Wolff, *General Editor*

CHARLES M. BRAND, the editor of this volume, is Associate Professor of History at Bryn Mawr College. He is the author of *Byzantium Confronts the West, 1180–1204,* and several articles on Islam and the Byzantine Empire.

Already Published

The Ancient World: Justice, Heroism, and Responsibility, *edited by Zeph Stewart,* S-141

Century of Genius: European Thought 1600–1700, *edited by Richard T. Vann,* S-149

The Crisis of Church & State, 1050–1300, *by Brian Tierney (with selected documents),* S-102

The English Reform Tradition, 1790–1910, *edited by Sydney W. Jackman,* S-120

The Enlightenment, *edited by Frank E. Manuel,* S-121

The French Revolution, *edited by Philip Dawson,* S-161

The Italian Renaissance, *edited by Werner L. Gundersheimer,* S-128

Nineteenth-Century Thought: The Discovery of Change, *edited by Richard L. Schoenwald,* S-129

The Protestant Reformation, *edited by Lewis W. Spitz,* S-140

Forthcoming Volumes

The Catholic Reformation, *edited by Theodore K. Rabb*

The Conversion of Western Europe, 350–750, *edited by J. N. Hillgarth*

The Image of Rome, *edited by Erich S. Gruen*

The Middle Ages, *edited by Archibald R. Lewis*

SOURCES OF CIVILIZATION IN THE WEST

Robert Lee Wolff, General Editor

[illegible]

ALREADY PUBLISHED

FORTHCOMING VOLUMES

ICON AND MINARET:

SOURCES OF BYZANTINE AND ISLAMIC CIVILIZATION

Edited by

Charles M. Brand

PRENTICE-HALL, INC.
Englewood Cliffs, New Jersey

 Library of Congress Catalog Card Number: 69–15332. Printed in the United States of America.

Current printing (last number):

10 9 8 7 6 5 4 3 2

Prentice-Hall International, Inc. (*London*)

For my parents,
Nan Surface Brand
and
Carl Fremont Brand

FOREWORD

"But I never even *heard* of Byzantium when I was in college," one is often told in a rather aggrieved tone of voice, by people who usually protest that they "adore history," and consider themselves well-educated. And the complaint does indeed truly reflect American academic practice, which in turn reflects—even if at several removes—the traditional attitudes of the academic profession. For them, Mediaeval history has all too often meant the history of Western Europe alone: the familiar story of the barbarian invasions of the Roman Empire; its disintegration into smaller regions that would later re-emerge as the national states of England, France, Germany, Italy, and so on; the uniting spiritual and cultural force of the Roman Catholic Church, and the characteristic feudal and manorial society, yielding only slowly to the development of industry and urbanism.

Gradually during recent decades, however, teachers and students of history have more generally become aware that at the eastern end of the Mediterranean the Roman Empire did not fall to the barbarians, but continued to thrive through many vicissitudes, during all the centuries that were "Mediaeval" for Western Europe. At Byzantium, or Constantinople, Constantine's city, dynasties of Roman Emperors succeeded each other. Greek was the popular, and before long the official, language; and Greek the literary and cultural tradition. Par excellence a Christian state and society, the Byzantine Empire resembled the Mediaeval West in many ways, but differed markedly from it in many others. There was much interchange, diplomatic and military, commercial, religious, and cultural, between them. We now recognize that to appreciate the Middle Ages we must make ourselves acquainted with both Eastern and Western European civilization, and that in the East the key is Byzantium. Bordering in the east on Byzantine territory and in Spain (and for a time in Sicily) on western Christian lands, the third great Mediaeval civilization of Islam also increasingly attracts our attention.

In this book, Professor Brand has skillfully selected from the wide range of Byzantine historical sources a series of passages from historians, biographers, and travellers, from the decrees of Church Councils, from the Lives of Saints, and from contemporary codes of law and imperial statutes that tell the reader what many aspects of Byzantine society were like; and in a short concluding section he introduces the reader to the religion and to some of the intellectual achievements of the Moslems. Some of these selections have never previously been translated into English, and are thus made available for the first time to those who do not read Byzantine Greek. This will, we hope, add a further sense of freshness for anyone who may here discover Byzantium and Islam for the first time, and enhance the experience for anyone who is seeking to improve an acquaintance already begun.

Robert Lee Wolff
Coolidge Professor of History
Harvard University

CONTENTS

Introduction

At the commencement of the Middle Ages, while Western Europe became a collection of barbarian kingdoms, the Near East retained a high level of culture and organization. Not until the twelfth century did the Latin-speaking world challenge the countries of the eastern Mediterranean. There the Byzantine Empire preserved the Greco-Roman heritage, and the Arabic Caliphates created a new civilization blended from the religion of Mohammed and the learning of classical Greece.

Strictly speaking, no such entity as the "Byzantine Empire" existed. The Roman Empire preserved an unbroken tradition from Augustus to Constantine XI, slain defending his capital in 1453; his subjects still called themselves "Romans." But at the start of the fourth century, after Diocletian had reorganized Roman institutions, Constantine I adopted Christianity and moved the capital to Byzantium on the Bosporus, renaming it Constantinople in his honor. In the fifth century the Latin-speaking half of the empire fell before the German onslaught, and Greek gradually became the language of emperors and subjects. This Christian, Greek-speaking remnant of the Roman Empire, with its distinctive blend of oriental, Greek, and Roman ideas, has been designated "Byzantine" by modern historians.

In the seventh century, the prophet Mohammed preached the monotheistic, puritanical religion of Islam to the nomads and traders of Arabia. Hitherto, this had been a desolate and backward land: now the Arabs, united under Mohammed's successors, the Caliphs, rushed forth to conquer in the name of religion the whole of the ancient Near East. The Persian Empire collapsed, and the weakened Byzantine state lost Syria, Palestine, Egypt, and ultimately North Africa, but survived in Asia Minor and the Balkans. Gradually a new organization, the theme system, whereby generals in command of army corps areas became provincial governors, replaced older Byzantine institutions. Despite territorial losses, Byzantine political and religious ideas maintained their sway.

The Byzantines believed that they existed to carry out God's will in the world. God intended all mankind to be Christian, to obey the commandments, and to be united under a single Byzantine emperor, God's representative on earth. Not only was the emperor responsible for the prosperity of the realm, but also for its spiritual welfare: he had to uphold orthodoxy and assist his subjects to achieve salvation. Councils of bishops, meeting under imperial guidance, defined doctrine, and numerous monasteries helped his people into heaven.

Constantinople, the heart of the empire, was one of the great cities of the medieval world, thickly populated, rich in treasure, and renowned for the holy relics in its churches. The city was therefore the target of many attacks, but it fell for the first time only in 1204 to the Christians of the Fourth Crusade, Venetian traders and French knights. Never could the Byzantines forget what seemed to them a treacherous blow. In 1261 the Palaeologus dynasty regained the city, only to lose it to the Mohammedan Turks.

The Arabs had already fallen victim to these same Turks. Outside Arabia, the Arab conquerors had blended with their subjects, while implanting their religion and usually their language. Native cultures and traditions gradually reasserted themselves, especially after a Persian family, the Abbasids, seized the Caliphate. Frontier regions became independent, and the Caliphs had by the late ninth century fallen under the control of their own guard-commanders. The eleventh-century advance of the Turks created a series of ephemeral principalities which usually lacked meaningful boundaries and political stability.

Such disintegration did little harm to Islamic civilization. The Abbasid era was one of great achievement, for the masterpieces of ancient Greece, now translated into Arabic, challenged outstanding scientific and philosophic thinkers. The conflict between reason and revelation, between Greek philosophy and the dogmas of the Koran, was protracted, but it ended with a victory for the forces of religious orthodoxy. Only in such neutral fields as social and political philosophy could Arabic thought advance.

Islam survives in the modern world as the religion of many millions; Byzantine political ideas and civilization were inherited by Russia and by the Orthodox churches of the East. In all of them old ideas and dreams have not entirely died.

Part One

BYZANTINE POLITICAL FOUNDATIONS

The Byzantine state inherited the autocratic tradition of Rome. On the Byzantine emperor, as on his Roman predecessor, rested the whole burden of the government, entailing final responsibility for all decisions and unlimited authority to execute them. Yet in practice he could work only within limits laid down by the traditions of the Roman-Byzantine state, especially those institutions and ideas embodied in Roman law: a "tyrant" risked speedy overthrow.

The Roman emperor had been regarded as divine, for only a god could govern so vast and heterogeneous a realm. When he accepted Christianity, Constantine the Great had to create a new conception of his relationship to God. His ideas were reflected and expounded by Eusebius, Bishop of Caesarea in Palestine. While scarcely a brilliant thinker, Eusebius shaped eastern Christian attitudes toward the state. As he explained to Constantine in an oration celebrating the commencement of Constantine's thirtieth year of rule (335), the emperor was directly chosen by God, and was thus blessed, inspired, and guided by God (see Reading No. 1).

After Eusebius, the Byzantines did not state their theories at great length; rather, the emperor's role was implicit in all that pertained to or emanated from him. Thus Constantine VII (called Porphyrogenitus, "Born-in-the-Purple"), in an oration to his generals (ca. 958), could refer to his subjects as his God-given heritage, his flock, and could even draw a parallel between himself and Christ (Reading No. 2). In the Preface to his *Book of Ceremonies,* he expanded this comparison: just as God rules the universe by the law of nature, so the emperor rules by the good order of the court—the empire is a model of the universe. In this selection, the essential word is *taxis,* which signifies both "right order" and "ritual"; for Constantine, the meanings are interchangeable, and their unavoidable separation in translation distorts his intention (Reading No. 3). From the last epoch of Byzantine history we have a description of the coronation in 1392 of Manuel II Palaeologus and Empress Helena. Throughout this text, the close relationship of the emperor to God is stressed. Indeed, the emperor appears here as a member of the priesthood, although the Byzantines avoided any precise definition of his status. Thus during one portion of the ceremonies he was clad as a bishop, and administered Communion to himself. Yet the people's role, by their acclamations, in the making of an emperor is also evident: it went back to a distant Roman past (Reading No. 4).

Once enthroned, the emperor had to act, for upon him depended the fate of the realm. A few examples will illustrate this point. The Byzantine Empire (as distinct from the Roman) originated in the conversion of Constantine I to Christianity. Eusebius gives an account of this momentous event in his *Life of Constantine,* which he composed after 337 on the basis of his conversations with the emperor (Reading No. 5). Not all Byzantine rulers were devoted or capable. Constantine IX Monomachus (1042–1055) gained the throne by marriage with Empress Zoe, who with her sister Theodora constituted the last survivors of the Macedonian Dynasty. A cultured man, patron of art and learning, Constantine IX indulged himself by introducing his mistress Sclerena into the palace and public life. His friend and secretary Michael Psellus in his *Chronographia* gives a picture of a luxurious court and carefree emperor (Reading No. 6). Partly as a result of Constantine IX's laxity, his successors found themselves in a difficult position. Alexius I Comnenus (1081–1118) was compelled at the outset of his reign to face Turks in Asia Minor, Petchenegs (a Turkic tribe) in Thrace, and Normans in the western Balkans. These last, under Robert Guiscard, had conquered the Byzantine possessions in southern Italy, and then, with the aid of a youth claiming to be the deposed Michael VII, had advanced upon Constantinople. Alexius I's bravery and skill in combating these enemies with limited forces inspired his daughter, Anna Comnena, to create an epic in prose, the *Alexiad.* Writing in the 1140s, in a nostalgic, hero-worshiping spirit, she utilized written sources and the recollections of her father's officials (Reading No. 7).

A. The Emperor Chosen by God

1. *Eusebius of Caesarea,* Tridecennial Oration (*A.D. 335*)

Eusebius of Caesarea, *The Oration of Eusebius Pamphilus, In Praise of the Emperor Constantine: Pronounced on the Thirtieth Anniversary of his Reign,* trans. Ernest C. Richardson, A Select Library of Nicene and Post-Nicene Fathers of the Christian Church, Second Series, Vol. I (New York: The Christian Literature Company, 1890), 584, 594–95, 606.

. . . Lastly, invested as he is with a semblance of heavenly sovereignty, he directs his gaze above, and frames his earthly government according to the pattern of that Divine original, feeling strength in its conformity to the monarchy of God. And this conformity is granted by the universal Sovereign to man alone of the creatures of this earth: for he only is the author of sovereign power, who decrees that all should be subject to the rule of one. And surely monarchy far transcends every other constitution and form of government: for that democratic equality of power, which is its opposite, may rather be described as anarchy and disorder. Hence there is one God, and not two, or three, or more: for to assert a plurality of gods is plainly to deny the being of God at all. There is one Sovereign; and his Word and royal Law is one: a Law not expressed in syllables and words, not written or engraved on tablets, and therefore subject to the ravages of time; but the living and self-subsisting Word, who himself is God, and who administers his Father's kingdom on behalf of all who are after him and subject to his power. . . .

. . . Such are the blessings resulting to mankind from this great and wondrous Sign, by virtue of which the evils which once existed are now no more, and virtues heretofore unknown shine everywhere resplendent with the light of true godliness. Discourses, and precepts, and exhortations to a virtuous and holy life, are proclaimed in the ears of all nations. Nay, the emperor himself proclaims them: and it is indeed a marvel that this mighty prince, raising his voice in the hearing of all the world, like an interpreter of the Almighty Sovereign's will, invites his subjects in every country to the knowledge of the true God. No more, as in former times, is the babbling of impious men heard in the imperial palace; but priests and pious worshipers of God together celebrate his majesty with royal hymns of praise. The name of the one Supreme Ruler of the universe is proclaimed to all: the gospel of glad tidings connects the human race with its Almighty King, declaring the grace and love of the heavenly Father to his children on the earth. His praise is everywhere sung in triumphant strains: the voice of mortal man is blended with the harmony of the angelic choirs in heaven; and the reasoning soul employs the body which invests it as an instrument for sounding forth a fitting tribute of praise and adoration to his name. The nations of the East and the West are instructed at the same moment in his precepts: the people of the Northern and Southern regions unite with one accord, under the influence of the same principles and laws, in the pursuit of a godly life, in praising the one Supreme God, in acknowledging his only begotten Son their Saviour as the source of every blessing, and our emperor as the one ruler on the earth, together with his pious sons. He himself, as a skillful pilot, sits on high at the helm of state, and directs the vessel with unerring course, conducting his people as it were with favoring breeze to a secure and tranquil haven. Meanwhile God himself, the great Sovereign, extends the right hand of his power from above for his protection, giving him victory over every foe, and establishing his empire by a lengthened period of years: and he will bestow on him yet higher blessings, and confirm in every deed the truth of his own promises. But on these we may not at present dwell; but must await the change to a better world: for it is not given to mortal eyes or ears of flesh, fully to apprehend the things of God.

And now, victorious and mighty Constantine, in this discourse, whose noble argument is the glory of the Almighty King, let me lay before thee some of the mysteries of his sacred truth: not as presuming to instruct thee, who art thyself taught of God; nor to disclose to thee those secret wonders which he himself, not through the agency of man, but through our common Saviour, and the frequent light of his Divine presence has long since revealed and unfolded to thy view: but in the hope of leading the unlearned to the light, and displaying before those who know them not the causes and motives of thy pious deeds. . . .

. . . At the same time one universal power, the Roman empire, arose and flourished, while the enduring and implacable hatred of nation against nation was now removed: and as the knowledge of one God, and one way of religion and salvation, even the doctrine of Christ, was made known to all mankind; so at the self-same period, the entire dominion of the Roman empire being vested in a single sovereign, profound peace reigned throughout the world. And thus, by the express appointment of the same God, two roots of blessing, the Roman empire, and the doctrine of Christian piety, sprang up together for the benefit of men. For before this time the various countries of the world, as Syria, Asia, Macedonia, Egypt, and Arabia, had been severally subject to different rulers. The Jewish people, again, had established their dominion in the land of Palestine. And these nations, in every village, city, and district, actuated by some insane spirit, were engaged in incessant and murderous war and conflict. But two mighty powers, starting from the same point, the Roman empire, which henceforth was swayed by a single sovereign, and the Christian religion, subdued and reconciled these contending elements. Our Saviour's mighty power destroyed at once the many governments and the many gods of the powers of darkness, and proclaimed to all men, both rude and civilized, to the extremities of the earth, the sole sovereignty of God himself. Meantime the Roman empire, the causes of multiplied governments being thus removed, effected an easy conquest of those which yet remained; its object being to unite all nations in one harmonious whole; an object in great measure already secured, and destined to be still more perfectly attained, even to the final conquest of the ends of the habitable world, by means of the salutary doctrine, and through the aid of that Divine power which facilitates and smooths its way.

2. *Constantine VII Porphyrogenitus,* Prologue to an Oration (*ca. A.D. 958*)

Address of the Emperor Constantine to the Generals of the East [ca. 958] from R. Vári, ed., "Zum historischen Exzerptenwerke des Konstantinos Porphyrogennetos," *Byzantinische Zeitschrift,* XVII (1908), 78–79. Translated by the editor.

It is desirable and pleasant to address you often without any probable cause, just as being deprived of converse with you is distressing and painful for myself and my judgment. For not thus do I care for and delight in my soldiers and think them worthy of every address and salutation, nor even to effect the same thing by writing to you, whom the only eternal and immortal God by His boundless mercy has entrusted to me as my portion and God-gathered people and the mightiest share of my lawful inheritance: but to me the pleasantest and most desirable [way] of all is to counsel you by word of mouth in matters of favor and obedience, and by words to teach and instruct [you] in matters of warfare, and to move toward courage the bolder persons fitted for this [warfare], as it is recognized and established that to rouse and stir the sluggish to courage and firmness is sweeter to me than every pleasure and delicacy. The holy words of the divine Gospel, which seek to show the greatness of God the Father's love for mankind, say: For God so loved the world that he gave his only begotten Son[1] unto death, but I hand over and crucify my whole self for you in body and soul and I mingle my flesh in your flesh and my bones in your bones and I consider each one of my limbs grown and created jointly with you, and I divide and distribute my soul itself as one substance for all of you, and for my part I wish to give life to and quicken my God-gathered people. Children, whom I have brought forth by the Gospel and have planted in the inheritance of God, God has exalted you and has led you into the midst of the most robust prime of life: receive the present advice sent you from the very depth of the soul and the hidden places of the heart. For, according to David who sings among the prophets, my heart and my flesh rejoiced in you.[2] And how should one not rejoice and skip and take delight when God has given unto His inheritance such armies, such a brave and most noble people, such champions and protectors of the Romans.

[1] John 3:16.

[2] Psalms 15:9 (Septuagint) = 16:9 (King James).

3. *Constantine VII Porphyrogenitus,* Preface to the Book of Ceremonies

Constantine VII Porphyrogenitus, *Le Livre des Cérémonies,* ed. Albert Vogt, Collection byzantine publiée sous le patronage de l'Association Guillaume Budé (Paris, 1935), I, pt. 1, 1–2. Translated by the editor.

A book and composition really worthy of imperial effort, by Constantine, Christ-loving emperor in Christ Himself the Eternal King, [and] son of Leo, wisest and ever-memorable emperor.

This task would seem excessive to others, who lack such care for necessary matters, but to us [it seems] very pleasant and desirable and more fitting than all other matters, since by this praiseworthy ritual imperial power appears better ordered and proceeds to better behavior and thereby is more admirable to foreigners and to our own people. For in the long course of time many things are known to cease, because they have been finished in it and exhausted by it, among which is that great and precious matter, the description and outline of imperial ritual; since it was overlooked and so to speak perishing, it was really possible to see the empire unadorned and ugly. For just as when a body is not gracefully shaped, one might call such a thing a confused and inharmonious disorder of limbs belonging to it, so when the imperial government is not guided and governed by ritual, it will differ in nothing from an individual and unpolished way of life. Lest this should happen, and being swept along in disorder we should seem to insult imperial grandeur, we have thought it necessary to collect by laborious care out of many places whatever was discovered by the ancients and reported by witnesses and seen by ourselves and instigated for us, and to set it forth in the present work for easy comprehension; also [we sought] to signal the transmission of forgotten ancestral customs to those after us, and to furnish them culled like flowers from meadows for incomparable beauty in imperial splendor, as if to establish some radiant and newly polished mirror amidst the palace, in which are reflected things befitting the imperial dignity and worthy of the senate, [in order that] the reins of power might be managed in good order and governance. So that the text might be clear and easily understood, we have used common and simple language and the same expressions and names which were formerly applied and uttered for each action. Thereby, since the imperial power is carried along in measure and good order, it would represent the Creator's harmony and activity concerning the whole [universe], and it would seem more dignified to the subjects and therefore more pleasing and admirable, [so] we must speak about each ceremony, how and in what manner it ought to be carried out and completed.

4. *Byzantine Coronation Ceremony: Manuel II and Helena Dragaš, 1392*

P. Schreiner, ed., "Hochzeit und Krönung Kaiser Manuels II. im Jahre 1392," *Byzantinische Zeitschrift,* LX (1967), 76–79. Translated by the editor.

[This fragment, apparently composed by a witness with an interest in liturgy, begins after Manuel II had been raised on a shield, had entered the Church of Haghia Sophia, and been clothed in purple:] . . . After censing the emperor when he approached the holy altar, one of the bishops took the crown [evidently the crown of the Caesar, a lower rank of the hierarchy, worn during the entry] from his head and gave it to the chief of the wardrobe. The patriarch took the incense-burner from the emperor's hands and censed the emperor himself. Then they left the altar and mounted to the pulpit, and there while the emperor bent his head the patriarch alone privately uttered a prayer—the bishops and deacons there heard him—which ran thus: "King of Kings and Lord of Lords, Who through Your prophet Samuel anointed Your servant David with holy oil as king and ruler of Your people, Yourself, holy Lord King, send down your power from Your holy abode through my sinful hands and anoint Your servant Manuel emperor and ruler of us, Your faithful people: bring forth in his days justice and the fullness of peace, subdue beneath his feet all foreign peoples who desire war, so that we who lead a quiet and harmless life may glorify Your splendid name by the supplications and prayers of Your all-holy Mother, of the holy and glorious prophet Samuel, and of the holy and glorious ancestor of God, the prophet David, of the holy and God-crowned great rulers and equals of the apostles Constantine [the Great] and Helen, and of all Your saints, because Thine is the kingdom and the power and the glory of Father and Son and Holy Spirit now and forever and unto ages of ages. Amen."

At once, in the hearing of the bishops and deacons in the pulpit [a large platform], the patriarch cried: "Holy, Holy, Holy," and in the hearing of all the people the archdeacon pronounced the threefold "Holy," and the whole people similarly the threefold "Holy," and again the patriarch [repeated] the triple "Holy," so the archdeacon and in succession the people, and again the patriarch, archdeacon, and people [cried] the triple "Holy," that is, the patriarch thrice [uttered] the triple "Holy," the archdeacon and people likewise. And he anointed him with unguent of nard and put a hood on him.

Then the patriarch placed the crown atop his head. But if the emperor is a son who has an emperor as father or an emperor is in office [i.e., if an emperor is crowning his son or someone else as co-emperor], the patriarch anoints him, but his father the emperor puts the crown on his head, and the whole people hail him. The patriarch gave him the cross in his right hand, and descending [from the pulpit] they stood at the throne. The empress, having approached, bent her head, and the crowned emperor, her husband, placed the crown customary for empresses upon her head, and gave into her right hand a golden scepter with precious stones and pearls.

Having worshiped at the altar and ascended the podium, they were seated on their thrones. The patriarch having approached the altar seated himself on [his] throne, and one of the deacons standing at the doors of the sanctuary [which was screened from the congregation by a wall called the iconostasis] uttered an acclamation of the rulers and the patriarch. And the whole people, as customary, hailed them with chanting. Behind the pulpit were two platforms made of wood: one on the right, the other on the left. On them stood the maïstores [i.e., masters] with the singers, wearing above their garments gold robes from the imperial wardrobe, directing the ceremonial, for this was their service. The chief singer and the musical director stood inactive at the throne, the lamp-bearer before the emperor with the double lamp below the imperial podium, and the leader of the service stood at the middle of the pulpit in its rearward part, and in a loud voice gave out the verses, and the maïstores sang for each verse in many voices, "Yea, holy," and then the verse. These were the verses:

Many years to you, rulers of the Romans,
Many years, Manuel, emperor of the Romans,
Many years, Helen, empress of the Romans,
This is the Lord's great day for the glory and
  acclamation of the Romans,
Glory, glory, glory to God in the highest and
  peace on earth, good will for men,
Glory to God Who has crowned you, rulers of
  the Romans.

And again they began, "Many years to you, rulers of the Romans," and the other verses aforesaid in succession. And they commenced them so that the beginning went from the [beginning of] divine liturgy up to the consecration [of the Eucharist]. They were silent at the time of the coronation, of the reading from the Apostle and from the holy Gospel, of the great entry [procession of clergy bearing the Eucharist to the altar], of the holy Eucharist, of the "Our Father," [and] of the elevation of the sacrament. Again they began:

Many, many years—unto many [years—a wish for long life]
Many years—unto many
Many years—unto many
Many years—unto many.

The [reading from the] Apostle was: "Brethren, receive the kingdom of God."[1] The Gospel [reading] was from the one according to John, "Whoever does not enter through the door into the sheepfold." [2]

When they should come for the great entry, the archdeacon emerging from the sanctuary summoned the emperor. The assembled deputatoi [an order of minor clerics] clad the emperor in a golden [episcopal] vestment and gave a staff into his right hand, and he advanced to the priests, and with him his guards. They came up to the throne and the emperor again turned back and ascending seated himself on his throne, while the priests advanced into the sanctuary.

After the elevation of the Eucharist, they called the emperor back

[1] Unidentified; evidently a paraphrase of Paul.

[2] John 10:1.

within the sanctuary, and entering he partook of the divine sacrament from his own hand and again returned to the podium.

When the dismissal [from the liturgy] came, the emperor rode on horseback from the church to the palace. From the church to the palace the highest dignitaries, to wit the despotai, sebastocrators, and caesars [members of the imperial family], on foot guided the bridles of the emperor's and empress' horses.

In the palace was prepared a podium, covered with scarlet cloth, with curtains in front of it; the whole populace was outside the curtains. The emperor with the empress seated themselves on the podium on their thrones; the maïstores exclaimed with chanting, "Appear, appear, appear, rulers of the Romans." And straightway drawing the curtains, the rulers appeared, and acclamation followed. When the curtains were closed again, the people lost sight of the rulers.

The emperor with the empress, entering the inner palace and putting on other garments, sat down at table. The dignitaries served them. The senators and other nobles of those reclining at the imperial table received [food] from the hands of the dignitaries. When the table was taken up, all, having done reverence [*proskynesis,* prostration], departed.

The chief chamberlain, having ascended to a high place which was prepared for the chamberlain, threw "little bundles" to the people. Within [each] cloth [bag] so given, called a "little bundle," were three gold pieces, three silver, and three bronze; these he threw to the people.

On the next day the emperor on horseback with the nobles completed the ceremony in the palace. For dinner the emperor with the empress dined seated on their thrones, and all the nobles in order dined before the emperor.

Such was the glorious ordination of the most holy emperor.

B. The Emperor in Action

5. *Eusebius of Caesarea,* Life of Constantine (*after A.D. 337*)

Eusebius of Caesarea, *The Life of the Blessed Emperor Constantine,* trans. Ernest C. Richardson, A Select Library of Nicene and Post-Nicene Fathers of the Christian Church, Second Series, Vol. I (New York: The Christian Literature Company, 1890), 488–93.

Flight of Constantine to His Father Because of the Plots of Diocletian.

The emperors then in power, observing his manly and vigorous figure and superior mind, were moved with feelings of jealousy and fear, and thenceforward carefully watched for an opportunity of inflicting some brand of disgrace on his character. But the young man, being aware of their designs, the details of which, through the providence of God, more than once came to him, sought safety in flight; in this respect again keeping up his resemblance to the great prophet Moses. Indeed, in every sense God was his helper; and he had before ordained that he should be present in readiness to succeed his father.

Death of Constantius, Who Leaves His Son Constantine Emperor

Immediately, therefore, on his escape from the plots which had been thus insidiously laid for him, he made his way with all haste to his father, and arrived at length at the very time that he was lying at the point of death. As soon as Constantius saw his son thus unexpectedly in his presence, he leaped from his couch, embraced him tenderly, and, declaring that the only anxiety which had troubled him in the prospect of death, namely, that caused by the absence of his son, was now removed, he rendered thanks to God, saying that he now thought death better than the longest life, and at once completed the arrangement of his private affairs. Then, taking a final leave of the circle of sons and daughters by whom he was surrounded, in his own palace, and on the imperial couch, he bequeathed the empire, according to the law of nature, to his eldest son, and breathed his last.

How, After the Burial of Constantius, Constantine Was Proclaimed Augustus by the Army.

Nor did the imperial throne remain long unoccupied: for Constantine invested himself with his father's purple, and proceeded from his father's palace, presenting to all a renewal, as it were, in his own person, of his father's life and reign. He then conducted the funeral procession in company with his father's friends, some preceding, others following the train, and performed the last offices for the pious deceased with an extraordinary degree of magnificence, and all united in honoring this thrice blessed prince with acclamations and praises, and while with one mind and voice, they glorified the rule of the son as a living again of him who was dead, they hastened at once to hail their new sovereign by the titles of Imperial and Worshipful Augustus, with joyful shouts. Thus the memory of the deceased emperor received honor from the praises bestowed upon his son, while the latter was pronounced blessed in being the successor of such a father. All the nations also under his dominion were filled with joy and inexpressible gladness at not being even for a moment deprived of the benefits of a well ordered government.

In the instance of the Emperor Constantius, God has made manifest to our generation what the end of those is who in their lives have honored and loved him. . . .

How He Resolved to Deliver Rome from Maxentius.

While, therefore, he regarded the entire world as one immense body, and perceived that the head of it all, the royal city of the Roman empire, was bowed down by the weight of a tyrannous oppression; at first he had left the task of liberation to those who governed the other divisions of the empire, as being his superiors in point of age. But when none of these proved able to afford relief, and those who had attempted it had experienced a disastrous termination of their enterprise, he said that life was without enjoyment to him as long as he saw the imperial city thus afflicted, and prepared himself for the overthrowal of the tyranny.

That After Reflecting on the Downfall of Those Who Had Worshiped Idols, He Made Choice of Christianity.

Being convinced, however, that he needed some more powerful aid than his military forces could afford him, on account of the wicked and magical enchantments which were so diligently practiced by the tyrant, he sought Divine assistance, deeming the possession of arms and a numerous soldiery of secondary importance, but believing the co-operating power of Deity invincible and not to be shaken. He considered, therefore, on what God he might rely for protection and assistance. While engaged in this enquiry, the thought occurred to him, that, of the many emperors who had preceded him, those who had rested their hopes in a multitude of gods, and served them with sacrifices and offerings, had in the first place been deceived by flattering predictions, and oracles which promised them all prosperity, and at last had met with an unhappy end, while not one of their gods had stood by to warn them of the impending wrath of heaven; while one alone who had pursued an entirely opposite course, who had condemned their error, and honored the one Supreme God during his whole life, had found him to be the Saviour and Protector of his empire, and the Giver of every good thing. Reflecting on this, and well weighing the fact that they who had trusted in many gods had also fallen by manifold forms of death, without leaving behind them either family or offspring, stock, name, or memorial among men: while the God of his father had given to him, on the other hand, manifestations of his power and very many tokens: and considering farther that those who had already taken arms against the tyrant, and had marched to the battle-field under the protection of a multitude of gods, had met with a dishonorable end (for one of them had shamefully retreated from the contest without a blow, and the other, being slain in the midst of his own troops, became, as it were, the mere sport of death); reviewing, I say, all these considerations, he judged it to be folly indeed to join in the idle worship of those who were no gods, and, after such convincing evidence, to err from the truth; and therefore felt it incumbent on him to honor his father's God alone.

How, While He Was Praying, God Sent Him a Vision of a Cross of Light in the Heavens at Mid-day, with an Inscription Admonishing Him to Conquer by That.

Accordingly he called on him with earnest prayer and supplications that he would reveal to him who he was, and stretch forth his right hand to help him in his present difficulties. And while he was thus praying with fervent entreaty, a most marvelous sign appeared to him from heaven, the account of which it might have been hard to believe had it been related by any other person. But since the victorious emperor himself long afterwards declared it to the writer of this history, when he was honored with his acquaintance and society, and confirmed his statement by an oath, who could hesitate to accredit the relation, especially since the tesimony of after-time has established its truth? He said that about noon, when the day was already beginning to decline, he saw with his own eyes the trophy of a cross of light in the heavens, above the sun, and bearing the inscription, CONQUER BY THIS. At this sight he himself was struck with amazement, and his whole army also, which followed him on this expedition, and witnessed the miracle.

How the Christ of God Appeared to Him in His Sleep, and Commanded Him to Use in His Wars a Standard Made in the Form of the Cross.

He said, moreover, that he doubted within himself what the import of this apparition could be. And while he continued to ponder and reason on its meaning, night suddenly came on; then in his sleep the Christ of God appeared to him with the same sign which he had seen in the heavens, and commanded him to make a likeness of that sign which he had seen in the heavens, and to use it as a safeguard in all engagements with his enemies.

The Making of the Standard of the Cross.

At dawn of day he arose, and communicated the marvel to his friends: and then, calling together the workers in gold and precious stones, he sat in the midst of them, and described to them the figure of the sign he had seen, bidding them represent it in gold and precious stones. And this representation I myself have had an opportunity of seeing.

A Description of the Standard of the Cross, Which the Romans Now Call the Labarum.

Now it was made in the following manner. A long spear, overlaid with gold, formed the figure of the cross by means of a transverse bar laid over it. On the top of the whole was fixed a wreath of gold and precious stones; and within this, the symbol of the Saviour's name, two letters indicating the name of Christ by means of its initial characters, the letter P being intersected by X in its centre: and these letters the emperor was in the habit of wearing on his helmet at a later period. From the cross-bar of the spear was suspended a cloth, a royal piece, covered with a profuse embroidery of most brilliant precious stones; and which, being also richly interlaced with gold, presented an indescribable degree of beauty to the beholder. This banner was of a square form, and the upright staff, whose lower section was of great length, bore a golden half-length portrait of the pious emperor and his children on its upper part, beneath the trophy of the cross, and immediately above the embroidered banner.

The emperor constantly made use of this sign of salvation as a safeguard against every adverse and hostile power, and commanded that others similar to it should be carried at the head of all his armies.

How Constantine Received Instruction, and Read the Sacred Scriptures.

These things were done shortly afterwards. But at the time

above specified, being struck with amazement at the extraordinary vision, and resolving to worship no other God save Him who had appeared to him, he sent for those who were acquainted with the mysteries of His doctrines, and enquired who that God was, and what was intended by the sign of the vision he had seen.

They affirmed that He was God, the only begotten Son of the one and only God: that the sign which had appeared was the symbol of immortality, and the trophy of that victory over death which He had gained in time past when sojourning on earth. They taught him also the causes of His advent, and explained to him the true account of His incarnation. Thus he was instructed in these matters, and was impressed with wonder at the divine manifestation which had been presented to his sight. Comparing, therefore, the heavenly vision with the interpretation given, he found his judgment confirmed; and, in the persuasion that the knowledge of these things had been imparted to him by Divine teaching, he determined thenceforth to devote himself to the reading of the Inspired writings.

Moreover, he made the priests of God his counselors, and deemed it incumbent on him to honor the God who had appeared to him with all devotion. And after this, being fortified by well-grounded hopes in Him, he hastened to quench the threatening fire of tyranny.

Of the Adulterous Conduct of Maxentius at Rome.

For he who had tyrannically possessed himself of the imperial city, had proceeded to great lengths in impiety and wickedness, so as to venture without hesitation on every vile and impure action.

For example: he would separate women from their husbands, and after a time send them back to them again, and these insults he offered not to men of mean or obscure condition, but to those who held the first places in the Roman senate. Moreover, though he shamefully dishonored almost numberless free women, he was unable to satisfy his ungoverned and intemperate desires. But when he assayed to corrupt Christian women also, he could no longer secure success to his designs, since they chose rather to submit their lives to death than yield their persons to be defiled by him.

How the Wife of a Prefect Slew Herself for Chastity's Sake.

Now a certain woman, wife of one of the senators who held the authority of prefect, when she understood that those who ministered to the tyrant in such matters were standing before her house (she was a Christian), and knew that her husband through fear had bidden them take her and lead her away, begged a short space of time for arraying herself in her usual dress, and entered her chamber. There, being left alone, she sheathed a sword in her own breast, and immediately expired, leaving indeed her dead body to the procurers, but declaring to all mankind, both to present and future generations, by an act which spoke louder than any words, that the chastity for which Christians are famed is the only thing which is invincible and indestructible. Such was the conduct displayed by this woman.

Massacre of the Roman People by Maxentius.

All men, therefore, both people and magistrates, whether of high or low degree, trembled through fear of him whose daring wickedness was such as I have described, and were oppressed by his grievous tyranny. Nay, though they submitted quietly, and endured this bitter servitude, still there was no escape from the tyrant's sanguinary cruelty. For at one time, on some trifling pretense, he exposed the populace to be slaughtered by his own body-guard; and countless multitudes of the Roman people were slain in the very midst of the city by the lances and weapons, not of Scythians or barbarians, but of their own fellow-citizens. And besides this, it is impossible to calculate the number of senators whose blood was shed with a view to the seizure of their respective estates, for at different times and on various fictitious charges, multitudes of them suffered death.

Magic Arts of Maxentius Against Constantine; and Famine at Rome.

But the crowning point of the tyrant's wickedness was his having recourse to sorcery: sometimes for magic purposes ripping up women with child, at other times searching into the bowels of newborn infants. He slew lions also, and practiced certain horrid arts for evoking demons, and averting the approaching war, hoping by these means to get the victory. In short, it is impossible to describe the manifold acts of oppression by which this tyrant of Rome enslaved his subjects: so that by this time they were reduced to the most extreme penury and want of necessary food, a scarcity such as our contemporaries do not remember ever before to have existed at Rome.

Defeat of Maxentius's Armies in Italy.

Constantine, however, filled with compassion on account of all these miseries, began to arm himself with all warlike preparation against the tyranny. Assuming therefore the Supreme God as his patron, and invoking His Christ to be his preserver and aid, and setting the victorious trophy, the salutary symbol, in front of his soldiers and body-guard, he marched with his whole forces, trying to obtain again for the Romans the freedom they had inherited from their ancestors.

And whereas, Maxentius, trusting more in his magic arts than in the affection of his subjects, dared not even advance outside the city gates, but had guarded every place and district and city subject to his tyranny, with large bodies of soldiers, the emperor, confiding in the help of God, advanced against the first and second and third divisions of the tyrant's forces, defeated them all with ease at the first assault, and made his way into the very interior of Italy.

Death of Maxentius on the Bridge of the Tiber.

And already he was approaching very near Rome itself, when, to save him from the necessity of fighting with all the Romans for the tyrant's sake, God himself drew the tyrant, as it were by secret cords, a long way outside the gates. And now those miracles recorded in Holy Writ, which God of old wrought against the ungodly (discredited by most as fables, yet believed by the faithful), did he in every deed confirm to all alike, believers and unbelievers, who were eye-witnesses of the wonders. For as once in the days of Moses and the Hebrew nation, who were worshipers of God, "Pharaoh's chariots and his host hath he cast into the sea, and his chosen chariot-captains are drowned in the Red Sea,"—so at this time Maxentius, and the soldiers and guards with him, "went down into the depths like stone," when, in his flight before the divinely-aided forces of Constantine, he essayed to cross the river which lay in his way, over which, making a strong bridge of boats, he had framed an engine of destruction, really against himself, but in the hope of ensnaring thereby him who was beloved by God. For his God stood by the one to protect him, while the other, godless, proved to be the miserable contriver of these secret devices to his own ruin. So that one might well say, "He hath made a pit, and digged it, and is fallen into the ditch which he made. His mischief shall return upon his own head, and his violence shall come down upon his own pate." Thus, in the present instance, under divine direction, the machine erected on the bridge, with the ambuscade concealed therein, giving way unexpectedly before the appointed time, the bridge began to sink, and the boats with the men in them went bodily to the bottom. And first the wretch himself, then his armed attendants and guards, even as the sacred oracles had before described, "sank as lead in the mighty waters." So that they who thus obtained victory from God might well, if not in the same words, yet in fact in the same spirit as the people of his great servant Moses, sing and speak as they did concerning the impious tyrant of old: "Let us sing unto the Lord, for he hath been glorified exceedingly: the horse and his rider hath he thrown into the sea. He is become my helper and my shield unto salvation." And again, "Who is like unto thee, O Lord, among the gods? who is like thee, glorious in holiness, marvelous in praises, doing wonders?"

6. *Michael Psellus,* Life of Constantine IX Monomachus *(1042–1055)*

Reprinted by permission of the publisher and the translator from Michael Psellus, *Fourteen Byzantine Rulers: The Chronographia of Michael Psellus,* trans. E. R. A. Sewter (Harmondsworth, England, and Baltimore, Md.: Penguin Books Ltd., 1966), pp. 162–64, 179, 180–85. Copyright © E. R. A. Sewter, 1966.

. . . Because of his family this man held very high rank in the Empire. He had the additional advantage of great wealth, and his personal appearance was singularly charming. Beyond all doubt he seemed a fit person to marry into the most illustrious families. In the first place he became son-in-law to the outstanding member of court society, but his wife fell ill and died. He was forced into a second alliance. At the time, Romanus, the future emperor, was still a private citizen, although high hopes were entertained that he would eventually be promoted and the people treated him with the greatest respect because of his position. Romanus had conceived a deep affection for Constantine —a young man in the flower of his manhood and scion of a most noble family—and he grafted this fine young cutting on his own rich fertile olive. The lady in question was none other than the daughter of his sister Pulcheria, who in the past had been married to Basil Sclerus (he had the misfortune later to be deprived of his sight) and had become the mother of this one child, a daughter. Alliance with this family conferred on the young man extraordinary brilliance, but he still held no important office. Basil's advisers, because of the hatred they nursed for the father, vented their spite on the son, and Sclerus's revolutionary designs had an unhappy effect on the emperor's relations with Constantine. That was the reason why neither Basil nor his brother Constantine ever promoted him to any responsible post in the government. They did him no actual harm, but he was slighted, and they certainly never dreamed that the man had a glorious future.

Even the accession of Romanus did little to help Constantine in his career, so mistaken was the new emperor in his estimate of the young man's qualities. However, Romanus did at least keep him at the imperial court, and, if for no other cause, he was very much in the public eye through his near relationship with the emperor. His fresh complexion (to the men of our generation he was as unspoiled as spring fruit) and his graceful manners and his conversation, in which he excelled all others, were the things that won the heart of the empress. She delighted in his company again and again. He for his part made himself thoroughly agreeable to her, and by cleverly adapting himself to please her on all occasions, he captivated her completely; by these arts he obtained favours from her, but at the same time both he and she were assailed with calumny from the court. There were times when their clandestine meetings were not much to the liking of most courtiers.

At any rate, these activities made him a likely candidate for promotion to the throne, and Michael (Romanus's successor) viewed him with suspicion. In fact, Michael, even after his own accession, remained stubbornly jealous, although not unfriendly at first. Later he trumped up false accusations, suborning witnesses unjustly, and Constantine was driven from the city. His punishment was relegation to a certain determined area, in this case the island of Mitylene (Lesbos), and there for seven years—the exact length of Michael's reign—he endured his misfortune. Michael Calaphates, like Paphlagon, inherited the emperors' hatred of the young man.

Zoe's first reaction, when for the second time she found herself at the head of the Empire, was, as I have already said, to protect herself against any sudden reversal of her good luck in the future. To strengthen her position she proceeded to look for a husband—not a man from abroad, but someone in the court circle. However, as one had been discredited through his calamity, another rejected because of his ignoble lineage, a third suspected as dangerous, and stories had been invented one after another to bring into disrepute her various suitors, she renounced all of them and again considered the claims of Constantine. She spoke openly on the subject to her personal bodyguard and household staff, and when she saw that they were unanimous in their support of him as the future emperor—their agreement seemed almost preconcerted—she informed the Senate also of her plans. These were greeted as an inspiration from God. So Constantine was recalled from his exile, and he set out, still a private citizen and without the paraphernalia of his new dignity. . . .

Constantine had no very clear conception of the nature of monarchy. He failed to realize that it entailed responsibility for the well-being of his subjects, and that an emperor must always watch over the administration of his realm and ensure its development on sound lines. To him the exercise of power meant rest from his labours, fulfilment of desire, relaxation from strife. He had entered the harbour of the palace, so to speak, to enjoy the advantages of a calm retreat and to avoid the duties of helmsman in the future. As for the administration of public affairs, and the privilege of dispensing justice, and the superintendence of the armed forces, they were delegated to others. Only a fraction of these duties was reserved for himself. Instead, he chose a life of pleasure and luxury, as if it were his natural right (not without some justification, for he had inherited an innate predilection for such things). Now, having acquired supreme power, he had greater opportunity for pleasure, and he indulged himself more than ever. . . .

Describing How and by What Means the Augusta Sclerena[1] Was Brought to the Capital.

It all came about in the following way. Constantine's second wife, a member of the famous Sclerus family, died, and, since he was at that time an ordinary citizen, he was prevented from marrying a third time, on conscientious grounds (by Roman law such marriages were illegal). But he substituted a less reputable condition for the marriage—a secret *affaire*. The lady in question was the niece of his late wife, a beautiful and normally a discreet woman. He induced her to share in this highly improper association. He may have bribed her; possibly he charmed her with words of love; or he may have used other methods of persuasion to achieve his purpose.

Whatever the reason, they were so much in love with each other that both found separation intolerable, even when they were threatened with misery, for when Constantine went into exile . . . this woman still remained at his side. With loving care she tended his wants, put at his disposal all her possessions, gave him all manner of comfort, and lightened the bitter load of his affliction. The truth is, she, no less than himself, was sustained by hopes of power; nothing else mattered if only in the future she might share the throne with her husband. I say "husband" because at that time she was convinced that their marriage would be legally sanctioned, and all her desires fulfilled when Constantine, as emperor, overruled the laws. When one of these ambitions was realized (his elevation to the throne), but circumstances did not permit the realization of the second, because the Empress Zoe seized all power for herself, she despaired altogether, not only of her cherished hopes, but even of life itself. The empress filled her with dread, and she anticipated grievous retribution.

Nevertheless, the emperor did not forget his beloved, even after his accession. With his physical eyes he beheld Zoe, but in his mind's eye was the image of his mistress; while he folded the empress in his arms, it was the other woman whom he clasped in the imagination of his heart. Regardless of the consequences, regardless of Zoe's jealousy,

[1] Niece of Pulcheria, sister of Romanus Sclerus, and grand-daughter of Bardas, she had shared Constantine's exile on Lesbos. She was unpopular with the people and because of her there was a riot during the emperor's procession to the Church of the Holy Martyrs (9 March 1044) and he barely escaped with his life.

turning a deaf ear to all entreaty, he brushed aside every counsel that would frustrate his wishes. Prominent among those who differed with him was his own sister Pulcheria, one of the cleverest women of our generation. She gave him excellent advice, but in vain, for he despised all opposition, and at his very first meeting with the empress spoke to her of this woman. He referred to her, not as a wife, nor as a prospective mistress, but as one who had suffered much at the hands of the imperial family. Moreover, she had endured, he said, much for his sake, and he begged Zoe to recall her from exile and grant her reasonable privileges.

The empress at once gave her consent. The fact is, Zoe was no longer jealous. She had had her own fill of trouble, and in any case she was now too old to harbour such resentment. Meanwhile, the emperor's beloved was expecting the worst, when suddenly there arrived messengers with an imperial bodyguard, summoning her back to Byzantium. They gave her letters, one from the emperor, the other from Zoe herself, promising a friendly reception and encouraging her to return. Such were the circumstances in which she arrived in the Queen of Cities.

At first it was considered proper that she should live in a modest house, with a bodyguard of no particular distinction. However, in order that he might have an excuse for going there often, Constantine treated it as a private residence of his own. Then, to give it an imposing appearance and make it a place fit to receive an emperor, he laid down new foundations for an annexe, with grand projects for the future.

He always had a pretext for these visits—that he was supervising some detail of the building—and several times a month he would go there, nominally to watch the progress of the work, but in reality to be with his mistress. He used to be accompanied by certain individuals of Zoe's faction, and lest they should busy themselves too much with his private affairs, he would see that a table loaded with delicacies was ready for them outside the house. They were invited to join in the banquet. The menu was chosen by themselves beforehand, and all their demands were satisfied. They were well aware of the real cause of these arrangements, but, for all their indignation at the way he treated their empress, it could not outweigh the pleasure they felt in the fulfilment of their own desires. Thus, if they knew Constantine was debating whether to visit his lady-love, but hesitating to set out and actually ashamed to go (and he usually was), they smoothed the path for him, each suggesting a different pretext. It was a singularly effective way of winning his favour.

At first, Constantine kept his assignations a secret, by visiting her in the way I have described, and he was still careful to avoid an open scandal. But gradually he lost all sense of impropriety and his real plans were revealed. All pretence of the lady's "apartment" in his house was abandoned. From now on he accompanied her quite openly, as often as he wished, and lived with her. If I may sum up the whole story before I continue, the liaison had a strange air of unreality about it. Whether one saw what was going on with one's own eyes or merely heard of it from others, it was hard to believe, for Constantine no longer visited the woman as a mistress, but as if she were in truth his wife.

He wasted the imperial treasures in satisfying her every whim. For example, he found in the palace a bronze casket, ornamented with figures carved in relief, and having filled it with money, sent it as a gift to her. Nor was this an occasional present, for there was a constant stream of such offerings to his beloved.

How the Augusta Was Introduced into the Palace.

So far, however, the love-affair was carried on in semi-secrecy. Yet efforts at concealment proved less and less effective as time went on, and eventually the emperor admitted publicly that he loved her. There followed an interview with Zoe, at which he proposed very plausibly that she should consent to live with his mistress. Even when Zoe agreed he was still not satisfied. A treaty of friendship was set out in a document and an imperial pavilion built for the ceremony of ratification. In front sat Zoe, Constantine, and Sclerena, while the Senate filed in to witness this extraordinary contract, blushing and for the most part talking in undertones. Despite their embarrassment, the senators still praised the agreement as if it were a document sent down from heaven. They called it a "loving-cup" and lavished on it all the other flattering epithets that deceive and cajole frivolous and empty-headed persons.

The contract being signed and the oaths administered, she who had hitherto been only a lover, was now introduced to the private apartments of the palace, no longer called "mistress," but "My Lady" and "Empress," officially. What was most astounding was the fact that, although most people were greatly distressed at the way in which Zoe had been deceived and neglected and despised, she herself evinced no emotion whatever, except that she smiled on everyone and apparently was quite pleased with the arrangement. At all events, she embraced her new partner with unusual warmth, and both of them accompanied the emperor. Both, too, discussed with him the same problems. Constantine weighed the judgement of each woman with equal impartiality, although it must be admitted that occasionally he allowed himself to be more readily influenced by his junior consort.

In appearance Sclerena was not specially remarkable. On the other hand, she was certainly no easy target for insult or raillery. As for her character and intellectual ability, she could charm a heart of stone, and she was amazingly adept in her interpretation of any matter whatever. Her speech was wonderful. It had a delicate beauty of expression, the rhythmic perfection of a scholar. There was in her conversation an unaffected sweetness of diction, an inexpressible grace in her manner of telling a story. She bewitched me, at any rate, when, as often happened, she would ply me with questions about the Greek myths and add a point here and there herself which she had learnt from some expert on the subject. No woman ever had a more sensitive ear, although I imagine this was not a natural accomplishment, but acquired because she knew that everyone was talking about her. She could hear a soft whisper quite clearly, and a word muttered under one's breath was readily understood by her.

I will give an example of this. One day, when we, the imperial secretaries, were all together, the empress's retinue was taking part in a procession. Zoe herself and her sister Theodora walked in this procession, followed by the Augusta (a new title granted her by the empresses, at the instigation of Constantine). As they were on their way—the route led them to the Theatre, and this was the first time the ordinary people had seen Sclerena in company with Zoe and Theodora—one of the subtle flatterers softly quoted Homer's "It were no shame . . ." [2] but did not complete the lines. At the time Sclerena gave no sign of having heard these words, but when the ceremony was over,

[2] Homer, *Iliad,* iii, 156–7, where the Trojans speak of Helen: "It were no shame that Trojans and well-greaved Achaeans should suffer pain long time for a woman such as she."

she sought out the man who had uttered them and asked him what they meant. She repeated his quotation without a single mistake, pronouncing the words exactly as he had whispered them. As soon as he told her the story in detail, and the crowd showed its approval of his interpretation of the anecdote, as well as of the Homeric reference, she was filled with pride and her flatterer was rewarded for his compliment. The presents she gave him were not a few, nor were they paltry trifles, but such as she was used to receiving and giving in her own circle. As a matter of fact, the emperor had given her a private fund for presents to individuals of either sex, in order to win the sympathies of the court, and especially of the two empresses.

7. *Anna Comnena,* Alexiad (*1140s*)

Reprinted by permission of the publishers, Routledge & Kegan Paul Ltd., London, and Barnes & Noble, Inc., New York, from Anna Comnena, *The Alexiad of the Princess Anna Comnena,* trans. Elizabeth A. S. Dawes (London: Kegan Paul, Trench, Trubner & Co., Ltd., 1928), pp. 89–91, 93–95.

Alexius saw that the Empire was nearly at its last gasp, for in the East the Turks were grievously harassing the frontiers whilst in the West things were very bad, as Robert was letting out every reef in his endeavour to foist that Pseudo-Michael, who had appealed to him, upon the throne. This was in my opinion only a pretext and it was rather the lust for power which inflamed him and allowed him no rest; consequently he used Michael as a Patroclus excuse and fanned the smouldering ashes of his ambition into a mighty flame and began arming himself with all his might against the Roman Empire. He prepared "dromones" and biremes and triremes and "sermones" and various kinds of freight-ships, fitting them out from the maritime districts and collecting as large forces as possible from the continent to further his purpose. Consequently the young and brave Emperor was desperate, and did not know which way to turn first, as each of his enemies seemed to be trying to begin war before the other, and thus he grew sorely vexed and disturbed. For the Roman Empire possessed only a very insufficient army (not more than the 300 soldiers from Coma, cowardly and inexperienced in war, besides just a few auxiliary barbarian troops, accustomed to carry their swords (?) on their right shoulder). And further there was no large reserve of money in the imperial treasury with which to hire allied troops from foreign countries. For the preceding Emperors had been very inefficient in all military and warlike matters and had thus driven the State of Rome into very dire straits. I myself have heard soldiers and other older men say that never within the memory of man had any State been reduced to such depths of misery. The Emperor's position was, as you can judge, very difficult and he was distracted by manifold anxieties. However, he was brave and fearless and had acquired great experience of war, so he determined to bring the Empire out of this heavy swell back to anchor by quiet shores, and with the help of God to beat these enemies who had arisen against him into empty foam, as waves are beaten when they break on rocks. He decided that first of all it was necessary to summon quickly all the local governors in the East who were holding forts and cities, and making a valiant resistance against the Turks. So he immediately drafted letters to them all; to Dabatenus, temporary governor of Heraclea in Pontus and of Paphlagonia; to Burtzes, governor of Cappadocia and Coma, and to the other leaders. He first set forth the occurrences which by God's providence had raised him to the imperial throne, and saved him miraculously from imminent danger, and secondly he bade them make provision for their respective districts to ensure their safety and leave sufficient soldiers for this purpose, and with the rest to present themselves at Constantinople and also bring up as many newly-recruited men in the prime of life as possible. Next he saw that he must take whatever steps were possible to guard himself against Robert and to try and deter the chieftains and counts who were flocking to the latter's standard. About this time the messenger returned, whom Alexius had dispatched before seizing the capital, to ask Monomachatus for help, and to beg him to forward some money. However the messenger only brought back letters detailing the reasons for which forsooth . . . Monomachatus could not help him as long as Botaniates still sat on the throne. After reading these letters Alexius was terrified lest on hearing of Botaniates' fall from the throne, Monomachatus should join Robert, and he became very despondent. He therefore sent for his brother-in-law, George Palæologus, and dispatched him to Dyrrachium (a city in Illyria) praying him to use every possible device for driving Monomachatus out of the town without fighting, since his forces were too small to eject him against his will, and to lay what counterplots he could to Robert's plots. He also ordered him to have the bulwarks remade in a new way with most of the nails that held the beams together left out so that if the Latins scaled them with ladders, directly they set foot on the beams, the latter, together with the men on them, would give way and be dashed to the ground below. He also wrote to the chiefs of the maritime districts and even to the islanders urging them not to lose courage nor to be careless but to watch and be sober, take measures for their protection and be on the look-out for Robert. Otherwise he might by a sudden descent upon them, make himself master of all the maritime towns, and even of the islands, and after that cause embarrassment to the Roman Empire.

Such then were the precautions taken by the Emperor for Illyria; and he seemed to have firmly secured the towns which at that moment lay directly in front, or at the feet, of Robert; nor was he unmindful of the districts which lay in his rear. Therefore he first sent a letter to Hermanus, Duke of Lombardy, next to the Pope of Rome, followed by one to Erbius, the Archbishop of Capua. Nay, he went even further and wrote to the princes, and to the various chiefs of the Frankish provinces, and by offering them moderate presents and by promising great gifts and dignities he tried to incite them to war against Robert. Some of these had already abandoned their alliance with Robert and others promised to do so, if they received further inducements! But as he knew that the King of Alamania was the most powerful of them all and could do whatever he liked against Robert, he wrote to him more than once, and tried to win him over by honeyed words and promises of all sorts. . . .

These were the measures he took for the Western part of the Empire and next he prepared himself against the immediate danger that threatened; he continued to reside in the capital, busily devising by what possible means he might resist the enemy who were almost at the very gates of the Empire. My history has already told how at this time the godless Turks were living round the Propontis and Solyman, the ruler of the whole of the East, was encamped around Nicæa (where he had his "sultanicium" corresponding to our "palace") and incessantly sending out raiders to devastate all the country round Bithynia and Thynia, and they made incursions on horse and on foot even as far as the Bosporus (now called Damalis), and carried off much booty, and they all but attempted crossing the sea itself. The Byzantines saw them living fearlessly in all the little towns along the coasts and in the sacred precincts even, as nobody drove them out, for the inhabitants were absolutely panic-stricken and did not know what steps to take. When the Emperor saw this, he hesitated between different plans, and often changed his mind and finally chose the plan which he considered the best and executed it as far as was possible. He had recently recruited soldiers from among the Romans and from Coma, from these he chose "decurions" and put them in command of boats with some light-armed troops who only carried their bows and a shield, and with others who according to their custom were fully armed with helmets, shields and spears. He instructed them to row along the coasts of the Propontis secretly during the night and to jump out and make an attack upon the infidels at any point where they noticed that the latter did not much outnumber themselves and then to run back quickly to their respective boats. As he knew that his men were quite inexpert in war, he told the rowers to row without making any noise, and also warned them to be on their watch against the infidels who would be in ambush in the clefts of the cliffs. After they had executed this manœuvre for several days, the barbarians did indeed gradually retire inland from the seaside districts. On being informed of this, the Emperor directed the soldiers to occupy the villages and buildings recently held by the Turks and to pass the night in them; and at break of day when for foraging or any other reason the enemy generally came out into the country, to make a sudden massed attack upon them, and be satisfied if they gained an advantage over them, however slight it might be, and not to risk restoring confidence to the enemy by seeking for further success, but to retire at once to the shelter of their forts. In consequence the barbarians after but a brief space of time again retreated to an even greater distance. Hereupon the Emperor gained courage, had the foot-soldiers put on horses and given spears to brandish, and made many cavalry raids upon the enemy, and no longer secretly during the night but in the daylight too. And those who had hitherto been decurions were now created captains over fifty and the men who had fought the enemy on foot at night with great fear now attacked them in early morning or at noon, and with confidence entered upon brilliantly successful engagements. Thus fortune now deserted the infidels and the power of the Roman Empire which had been temporarily obscured shone forth. For Comnenus not only drove them far back from the Bosporus and the whole seaboard, but also routed them out of the whole of Bithynia, Thynia and the province of Nicomedia and reduced the sultan to making urgent overtures for peace. As Alexius was hearing from many quarters of the tremendous onset Robert was preparing and of the immense number of troops he had collected, and that he was hastening on his march to the coast of Lombardy, he gladly received the proposal of peace. For, if even the hero Heracles could not fight two men at the same time, as the proverb suggests, much less could this young ruler, who possessed neither forces nor money and had only just taken over a state already corrupt which had for a long time been gradually diminishing and had sunk practically to the lowest depths; and all its money had been squandered without any useful result. This was the reason he felt himself compelled to agree to terms of peace after, by various methods, chasing the Turks away from Damalis and its coasts, and further buying them off with bribes. He fixed the river called Dracon as their boundary, and compelled them to promise never to cross it or make incursions into Bithynian territory.

Part Two

BYZANTINE SPIRITUAL FOUNDATIONS

Unlike modern states, the Byzantine Empire was not a purely secular institution. Deeming themselves the chosen instruments of God for the organization of mankind into a single realm, emperors and people agreed that the Byzantine state existed to achieve a spiritual goal. Armies and government strove to maintain peace and order so that the individual might be free to work out the salvation of his soul. The earlier Roman ideal of affording peace with justice to all was thus elevated to a new plane. A statement of this Byzantine sense of purpose occurs in the patriarch's prayer in the coronation ritual for Manuel II (see above, Reading No. 4).

The emperor deemed himself responsible to God for the spiritual well-being of his people. Correct Christian doctrine (*orthe doxa* or orthodoxy) had to be maintained; failure to do so would alienate the empire from God. Constantine I felt bound to enforce (and even to determine) true doctrine. When in 324 he seized the eastern half of the empire, he found the Christian population divided between followers of Arius (who maintained that Christ was different from, and therefore less than, God the Father) and his opponents, led by Bishop Alexander of Alexandria. After urging peace upon both parties (Reading No. 8), Constantine held a council of bishops at Nicaea in 325. The emperor himself presided, and, as Eusebius reports in a letter composed shortly afterward, he dictated the solution of the problem, the definition of Christ as "of the same substance" (*homoousios*) as the Father. He even explained the meaning of the word to the council, and the bishops perforce accepted the emperor's view (Reading No. 9). This supervision over doctrine, together with the emperor's assumed right to nominate bishops and govern the church, is called Caesaropapism. But state control was regarded by the Byzantines as in the service of God, true doctrine, and the church. Rarely did individuals object, and usually they spoke from self-interest rather than for an abstract ideal of separation of church and state.

Later emperors repeatedly convened councils to resolve other religious disputes, although they seldom directed the bishops as firmly as Constantine had. Nor did all decisions find acceptance: the decrees of the Second Council of Ephesus (449), while supported by Emperor Theodosius II, met with widespread hostility. Theodosius' successor, Marcian, hastened to reverse them at the Council of Chalcedon (451). The point in dispute concerned the relationship of the divine and human natures in Christ: many Syrians and Egyptians believed that Christ's human nature was subsumed in His divine one, so that the incarnate Christ had only a single divine nature (they were called Monophysites, "one-nature believers"). The Council of Chalcedon, however, taught that Christ had two complete natures, divine and human, and defined their relationship (Reading No. 10).

The sources of Orthodox doctrine included the Bible, the Fathers of the Church (Athanasius and John Chrysostom, for example), and also tradition, the beliefs and practices of the Christian populace. An important aspect of eastern Christian tradition was challenged by the Iconoclast emperors. Byzantines had for a long time offered prayers to images of Christ, the Virgin (called "Theotokos," "Mother of God," by the Byzantines), and the saints, in the belief that the persons depicted would intercede with God for the suppliant. The image thus became a channel of communication with God. The Iconoclasts ("image-breakers"), who desired a purified religion, wished to expel all images save the Cross itself from churches, shrines, and private homes. In 726 Leo III abolished the cult of images by imperial edict; not until 754 did his successor hold a council to approve this doctrine. But in 787 the empress-mother Irene, a supporter of the images and regent for her young son, held at Nicaea the Seventh Ecumenical Council. At her bidding, the bishops annulled the decrees of 754 and reestablished the veneration (not the worship) of images (Reading No. 11).

If the emperor's power to decree doctrine thus became somewhat limited, he still remained the principal defender of Orthodoxy. Among the heretics whom Byzantines had to combat were the Paulicians or Bogomils; their ideas descended from earlier Manichaeanism. In the view of the Bogomils, the world and mankind had been created by Satan, although man also had a portion of God-given life. The Christian Church and the imperial government were works of the Evil One. The best thing a man could do was to purify himself by asceticism and render his life back to God. Bogomils attracted popular support by their way of life and their contempt for the religious hierarchy and the government. No emperor was more vigorous in repressing them than Alexius I; Anna Comnena proudly records how in 1109–1111 he trapped the Bogomil leader Basil (Reading No. 12).

But the preservation of external correctness in doctrine was only part of the Byzantine religious program. Christianity sought to awaken men spiritually, and the empire existed to assist men to salvation. Monasticism became a primary vehicle in achieving these purposes. Not only did a monk, because of his separation from worldly temptation, improve his chance of salvation, but monks also served as spiritual guides for laymen. An individual could seek help for his inner life, and emperors often consulted ascetics on matters of high policy. The prosperity of the empire was measured more by the spiritual men it contained than by its material wealth.

The pattern of Byzantine (and also Western) asceticism was found in the person of St. Anthony (ca. 250–356), an obscure Egyptian hermit who became a spiritual lamp to the world. His biography, written soon after his death by his friend St. Athanasius, influenced all later ascetics (Reading No. 13). But Anthony, although he allowed followers to gather around him, had been an individualist. Since many persons found themselves unable to carry out a lifelong program of private asceticism, there arose the practice of living together in monasteries under an abbot. For the institution he founded about 360 in Asia Minor, St. Basil of Caesarea (in Cappadocia) prepared the dialogue on monastic life called *The Long Rules* (Reading No. 14). Basil stressed the value of communal existence. His writings guided Byzantine (and later Russian) monks, and St. Benedict used them in preparing a Latin rule.

A. The Quest for Orthodoxy

8. *Eusebius of Caesarea,* Life of Constantine

Eusebius of Caesarea, *The Life of the Blessed Emperor Constantine,* trans. Ernest C. Richardson, A Select Library of Nicene and Post-Nicene Fathers of the Christian Church, Second Series, Vol. I (New York: The Christian Literature Company, 1890), 515–18.

How Controversies Originated at Alexandria Through Matters Relating to Arius.

In this manner the emperor, like a powerful herald of God, addressed himself by his own letter to all the provinces, at the same time warning his subjects against superstitious error, and encouraging them in the pursuit of true godliness. But in the midst of his joyful anticipations of the success of this measure, he received tidings of a most serious disturbance which had invaded the peace of the Church. This intelligence he heard with deep concern, and at once endeavored to devise a remedy for the evil. The origin of this disturbance may be thus described. The people of God were in a truly flourishing state, and abounding in the practice of good works. No terror from without assailed them, but a bright and most profound peace, through the favor of God, encompassed his Church on every side. Meantime, however, the spirit of envy was watching to destroy our blessings, which at first crept in unperceived, but soon revelled in the midst of the assemblies of the saints. At length it reached the bishops themselves, and arrayed them in angry hostility against each other, on pretense of a jealous regard for the doctrines of Divine truth. Hence it was that a mighty fire was kindled as it were from a little spark, and which, originating in the first instance in the Alexandrian church, overspread the whole of Egypt and Libya, and the further Thebaid. Eventually it extended its ravages to the other provinces and cities of the empire; so that not only the prelates of the churches might be seen encountering each other in the strife of words, but the people themselves were completely divided, some adhering to one faction and others to another. Nay, so notorious did the scandal of these proceedings become, that the sacred matters of inspired teaching were exposed to the most shameful ridicule in the very theaters of the unbelievers. . . .

CONSTANTINE'S LETTER TO ALEXANDER THE BISHOP, AND ARIUS THE PRESBYTER. . . . ORIGIN OF THE CONTROVERSY BETWEEN ALEXANDER AND ARIUS, AND THAT THESE QUESTIONS OUGHT NOT TO HAVE BEEN DISCUSSED.

"I understand, then, that the origin of the present controversy is this. When you, Alexander, demanded of the presbyters what opinion they severally maintained respecting a certain passage in the Divine law, or rather, I should say, that you asked them something connected with an unprofitable question, then you, Arius, inconsiderately insisted on what ought never to have been conceived at all, or if conceived, should have been buried in profound silence. Hence it was that a dissension arose between you, fellowship was withdrawn, and the holy people, rent into diverse parties, no longer preserved the unity of the one body. Now, therefore, do ye both exhibit an equal degree of forbearance, and receive the advice which your fellow-servant righteously gives. What then is this advice? It was wrong in the first instance to propose such questions as these, or to reply to them when propounded. For those points of discussion which are enjoined by the authority of no law, but rather suggested by the contentious spirit which is fostered by misused leisure, even though they may be intended merely as an intellectual exercise, ought certainly to be confined to the region of our own thoughts, and not hastily produced in the popular assemblies, nor unadvisedly intrusted to the general ear. For how very few are there able either accurately to comprehend, or adequately to explain subjects so sublime and abstruse in their nature? Or, granting that one were fully competent for this, how many people will he convince? Or, who, again, in dealing with questions of such subtle nicety as these, can secure himself against a dangerous declension from the truth? It is incumbent therefore on us in these cases to be sparing of our words, lest, in case we ourselves are unable, through the feebleness of our natural faculties, to give a clear explanation of the subject before us, or, on the other hand, in case the slowness of our hearers' understandings disables them from arriving at an accurate apprehension of what we say, from one or other of these causes the people be reduced to the alternative either of blasphemy or schism.

An Exhortation to Unanimity.

"Let therefore both the unguarded question and the inconsiderate answer receive your mutual forgiveness. For the cause of your difference has not been any of the leading doctrines or precepts of the Divine law, nor has any new heresy respecting the worship of God arisen among you. You are in truth of one and the same judgment: you may therefore well join in communion and fellowship.

There Should Be No Contention in Matters Which Are in Themselves of Little Moment.

"For as long as you continue to contend about these small and very insignificant questions, it is not fitting that so large a portion of God's people should be under the direction of your judgment, since you are thus divided between yourselves. I believe it indeed to be not merely unbecoming, but positively evil, that such should be the case. But I will refresh your minds by a little illustration, as follows. You know that philosophers, though they all adhere to one system, are yet frequently at issue on certain points, and differ, perhaps, in their degree of knowledge: yet they are recalled to harmony of sentiment by the uniting power of their common doctrines. If this be true, is it not far more reasonable that you, who are the ministers of the Supreme God, should be of one mind respecting the profession of the same religion? But let us still more thoughtfully and with closer attention examine what I have said, and see whether it be right that, on the ground of some trifling and foolish verbal difference between ourselves, brethren should assume towards each other the attitude of enemies, and the august meeting of the Synod be rent by profane disunion, because of you who wrangle together on points so trivial and altogether unessential? This is vulgar, and rather characteristic of childish ignorance, than consistent with the wisdom of priests and men of sense. Let us withdraw ourselves with a good will from these temptations of the devil. Our great God and common Saviour of all has granted the same light to us all. Permit me, who am his servant, to bring my task to a successful issue, under the direction of his Providence, that I may be enabled, through my exhortations, and diligence, and earnest admonition, to recall his people to communion and fellowship. For since you have, as I said, but one faith, and one sentiment respecting our religion, and since the Divine commandment in all its parts enjoins on us all the duty of maintaining a spirit of concord, let not the circumstance which has led to a slight difference between you, since it does not affect the validity of the whole, cause any division or schism among you. And this I say without in any way desiring to force you to entire unity of judgment in regard to this truly idle question, whatever its real nature may be. For the dignity of your synod may be preserved, and the communion of your whole body maintained unbroken, however wide a difference may exist among you as to unimportant matters. For we are not all of us like-minded on every subject, nor is there such a thing as one disposition and judgment common to all alike. As far, then, as regards the Divine Providence, let there be one faith, and one understanding among you, one united judgment in reference to God. But as to your subtle disputations on questions of little or no significance, though you may be unable to harmonize in sentiment, such differences should be consigned to the secret custody of your own minds and thoughts. And now, let the preciousness of common affection, let faith in the truth, let the honor due to God and to the observance of his law continue immovably among you. Resume, then, your mutual feelings of friendship, love, and regard: restore to the people their wonted embracings; and do ye yourselves, having purified your souls, as it were, once more acknowledge one another. For it often happens that when a reconciliation is effected by the removal of the causes of enmity, friendship becomes even sweeter than it was before.

THE EXCESS OF HIS PIOUS CONCERN CAUSED HIM TO SHED TEARS; AND HIS INTENDED JOURNEY TO THE EAST WAS POSTPONED BECAUSE OF THESE THINGS.

"Restore me then my quiet days, and untroubled nights, that the joy of undimmed light, the delight of a tranquil life, may henceforth be my portion. Else must I needs mourn, with constant tears, nor shall I be able to pass the residue of my days in peace. For while the people of God, whose fellow-servant I am, are thus divided amongst themselves by an unreasonable and pernicious spirit of contention, how is it possible that I shall be able to maintain tranquillity of mind? And I will give you a proof how great my sorrow has been on this behalf. Not long since I had visited Nicomedia, and intended forthwith to proceed from that city to the East. It was while I was hastening towards you, and had already accomplished the greater part of the distance, that the news of this matter reversed my plan, that I might not be compelled to see with my own eyes that which I felt myself scarcely able even to hear. Open then for me henceforward by your unity of judgment that road to the regions of the East which your dissensions have closed against me, and permit me speedily to see yourselves and all other peoples rejoicing together, and render due acknowledgment to God in the language of praise and thanksgiving for the restoration of general concord and liberty to all."

THE CONTROVERSY CONTINUES WITHOUT ABATEMENT, EVEN AFTER THE RECEIPT OF THIS LETTER.

In this manner the pious emperor endeavored by means of the foregoing letter to promote the peace of the Church of God. And the excellent man to whom it was intrusted performed his part not merely by communicating the letter itself, but also by seconding the views of him who sent it; for he was, as I have said, in all respects a person of pious character. The evil, however, was greater than could be remedied by a single letter, insomuch that the acrimony of the contending parties continually increased, and the effects of the mischief extended to all the Eastern provinces. These things jealousy and some evil spirit who looked with an envious eye on the prosperity of the Church, wrought.

9. *Eusebius of Caesarea,* Letter on the Council of Nicaea

Eusebius of Caesarea, "Letter on the Council of Nicaea," in Socrates Scholasticus, *The Ecclesiastical History,* trans. A. C. Zenos, A Select Library of Nicene and Post-Nicene Fathers of the Christian Church, Second Series, Vol. II (New York: The Christian Literature Company, 1890), 10–12.

"You have probably had some intimation, beloved, of the transactions of the great council convened at Nicæa, in relation to the faith of the Church, inasmuch as rumor generally outruns true account of that which has really taken place. But lest from such report alone you might form an incorrect estimate of the matter, we have deemed it necessary to submit to you, in the first place, an exposition of the faith proposed by us in written form; and then a second which has been promulgated, consisting of ours with certain additions to its expression. The declaration of faith set forth by us, which when read in the presence of our most pious emperor, seemed to meet with universal approbation, was thus expressed:

" 'According as we received from the bishops who preceded us, both in our instruction [in the knowledge of the truth], and when we were baptized; as also we have ourselves learned from the sacred Scriptures: and in accordance with what we have both believed and taught while discharging the duties of presbyter and the episcopal office itself, so now we believe and present to you the distinct avowal of our faith. It is this:

" 'We believe in one God, the Father Almighty, Maker of all things visible and invisible:—and in one Lord, Jesus Christ, the Word of God, God of God, Light of light, Life of life, the only-begotten Son, born before all creation, begotten of God the Father, before all ages, by whom also all things were made; who on account of our salvation became incarnate, and lived among men; and who suffered and rose again on the third day, and ascended to the Father, and shall come again in glory to judge the living and the dead. We believe also in one Holy Spirit. We believe in the existence and subsistence of each of these [persons]: that the Father is truly Father, the Son truly Son, and the Holy Spirit truly Holy Spirit; even as our Lord also, when he sent forth his disciples to preach the Gospel, said, "Go and teach all nations, baptizing them in the name of the Father, and of the Son, and of the Holy Spirit." Concerning these doctrines we steadfastly maintain their truth, and avow our full confidence in them; such also have been our sentiments hitherto, and such we shall continue to hold until death: and in an unshaken adherence to this faith, we anathematize every impious heresy. In the presence of God Almighty, and of our Lord Jesus Christ we testify, that thus we have believed and thought from our heart and soul, since we have possessed a right estimate of ourselves; and that we now think and speak what is perfectly in accordance with the truth. We are moreover prepared to prove to you by undeniable evidences, and to convince you that in time past we have thus believed, and so preached.'

"When these articles of faith were proposed, there seemed to be no ground of opposition: nay, our most pious emperor himself was the first to admit that they were perfectly correct, and that he himself had entertained the sentiments contained in them; exhorting all present to give them their assent, and subscribe to these very articles, thus agreeing in a unanimous profession of them, with the insertion, however, of that single word *'homoousios'* (consubstantial), an expression which the emperor himself explained, as not indicating corporeal affections or properties; and consequently that the Son did not subsist from the Father either by division or abscission: for, said he, a nature which is immaterial and incorporeal cannot possibly be subject to any corporeal affection; hence our conception of such things can only be in divine and mysterious terms. Such was the philosophical view of the subject taken by our most wise and pious sovereign; and the bishops on account of the word *homoousios,* drew up this formula of faith.

THE CREED.

" 'We believe in one God, the Father Almighty, Maker of all things visible and invisible:—and in one Lord Jesus Christ, the Son of God, the only-begotten of the Father, that is of the substance of the

Father; God of God, Light of light, true God of true God; begotten not made, consubstantial with the Father; by whom all things were made both which are in heaven and on earth; who for the sake of us men, and on account of our salvation, descended, became incarnate, was made man, suffered and rose again on the third day; he ascended into the heavens, and will come to judge the living and the dead. [We believe] also in the Holy Spirit. But those who say "There was a time when he was not," or "He did not exist before he was begotten," or "He was made of nothing," or assert that "He is of other substance or essence than the Father," or that the Son of God is created, or mutable, or susceptible of change, the Catholic and apostolic Church of God anathematizes.'

"Now this declaration of faith being propounded by them, we did not neglect to investigate the distinct sense of the expressions 'of the substance of the Father, and consubstantial with the Father.' Whereupon questions were put forth and answers, and the meaning of these terms was clearly defined; when it was generally admitted that *ousias* (of the essence or substance) simply implied that the Son is of the Father indeed, but does not subsist as a part of the Father. To this interpretation of the sacred doctrine which declares that the Son is of the Father, but is not a part of his substance, it seemed right to us to assent. We ourselves therefore concurred in this exposition; nor do we cavil at the word '*homoousios*' having regard to peace, and fearing to lose a right understanding of the matter. On the same grounds we admitted also the expression 'begotten, not made': 'for *made*,' said they, 'is a term applicable in common to all the creatures which were made by the Son, to whom the Son has no resemblance. Consequently he is no creature like those which were made by him, but is of a substance far excelling any creature; which substance the Divine Oracles teach was begotten of the Father by such a mode of generation as cannot be explained nor even conceived by any creature.' Thus also the declaration that 'the Son is consubstantial with the Father' having been discussed, it was agreed that this must not be understood in a corporeal sense, or in any way analogous to mortal creatures; inasmuch as it is neither by division of substance, nor by abscission, nor by any change of the Father's substance and power, since the underived nature of the Father is inconsistent with all these things. That he is consubstantial with the Father then simply implies, that the Son of God has no resemblance to created things, but is in every respect like the Father only who begat him; and that he is of no other substance or essence but of the Father. To which doctrine, explained in this way, it appeared right to assent, especially since we knew that some eminent bishops and learned writers among the ancients have used the term *'homoousios'* in their theological discourses concerning the nature of the Father and the Son. Such is what I have to state to you in reference to the articles of faith which have been promulgated; and in which we have all concurred, not without due examination, but according to the senses assigned, which were investigated in the presence of our most highly favored emperor, and for the reasons mentioned approved. We have also considered the anathema pronounced by them after the declaration of faith inoffensive; because it prohibits the use of illegitimate terms, from which almost all the distraction and commotion of the churches have arisen. Accordingly, since no divinely inspired Scripture contains the expressions, 'of things which do not exist,' and 'there was a time when he was not,' and such other phrases as are therein subjoined, it seemed unwarrantable to utter and teach them: and moreover this decision received our sanction the rather from the consideration that we have never heretofore been accustomed to employ these terms. We deemed it incumbent on us, beloved, to acquaint you with the caution which has characterized both our examination of and concurrence in these things: and that on justifiable grounds we resisted to the last moment the introduction of certain objectionable expressions as long as these were not acceptable; and received them without dispute, when on mature deliberation as we examined the sense of the words, they appeared to agree with what we had originally proposed as a sound confession of faith."

10. *Decree of the Council of Chalcedon (451)*

Following the holy Fathers, we all with one voice teach men to confess that the Son and our Lord Jesus Christ is one and the same, that He is perfect in godhead and perfect in manhood, truly God and truly man, of a reasonable soul and body, consubstantial with His Father as touching His godhead, and consubstantial with us as to His manhood, in all things like unto us, without sin; begotten of His Father before all worlds according to His godhead; but in these last days for us and for our salvation of the Virgin Mary, the Theotokos, according to His manhood, one and the same Christ, Son, Lord, only begotten Son, in two natures, unconfusedly, immutably, indivisibly, inseparably; the distinction of natures being preserved and concurring in one person and hypostasis, not separated or divided into two persons, but one and the same Son and Only begotten, God the Word, the Lord Jesus Christ, as the prophets from the beginning have spoken concerning Him, and as the Lord Jesus Christ himself has taught us, and as the creed of the Fathers has delivered us.

11. *Decree of the Second Council of Nicaea (787)*

Reprinted with the permission of Charles Scribner's Sons from *A Source Book for Ancient Church History*, pp. 696–97, by Joseph C. Ayer, Jr. Copyright 1913 Charles Scribner's Sons; renewal copyright 1941 Joseph Cullen Ayer, Jr.

We, therefore, following the royal pathway and the divinely inspired authority of our holy Fathers and the traditions of the Catholic Church for, as we all know, the Holy Spirit dwells in her, define with all certitude and accuracy, that just as the figure of the precious and life-giving cross, so also the venerable and holy images, as well in painting and mosaic, as of other fit materials, should be set forth in the holy churches of God, and on the sacred vessels and on the vestments and on hangings and in tablets both in houses and by the wayside, to wit, the figure of our Lord God and Saviour Jesus Christ, of our spotless lady, the Theotokos, of the venerable angels, of all saints, and of all pious people. For by so much the more frequently as they are seen in artistic representation, by so much the more readily are men lifted up to the memory of their prototypes, and to a longing after them; and to these should be given due salutation and honorable reverence [ἀσπασμὸν καὶ τιμητικὴν προσκύνησιν], not indeed that true worship [τὴν ἀληθινὴν λατρείαν] which pertains alone to the divine nature; but to these, as to the figure of the precious and life-giving cross, and to the book of the Gospels and to other holy objects, incense and lights may be offered according to ancient pious custom. For the honor which is paid to the image passes on to that which the image represents, and he who shows reverence [προσκυνεῖ] to the image shows reverence to the subject represented in it. For thus the teaching of our holy Fathers, which is called the tradition of the Catholic Church, which from one end of the earth to the other hath received the Gospel, is strengthened. Thus we follow Paul, who spake in Christ, and the whole divine Apostolic company and the holy Fathers, holding fast the traditions which we have received. So we sing prophetically the triumphal hymns of the Church: Rejoice greatly, O daughter of Sion; Shout, O daughter of Jerusalem. Rejoice and be glad with all thy heart. The Lord hath taken away from thee the oppression of thy adversaries; thou art redeemed from the hand of thy enemies: The Lord is a king in the midst of thee; thou shalt not see evil any more, and peace be unto thee forever.

Those, therefore, who dare to think or teach otherwise, or as wicked heretics dare to spurn the traditions of the Church and to invent some novelty, or else to reject some of those things which the Church hath received, to wit, the book of the Gospels, or the image of the cross, or the pictorial icons, or the holy relics of a martyr, or evilly and sharply to devise anything subversive of the lawful traditions of the Catholic Church, or to turn to common uses the sacred vessels and the venerable monasteries, if they be bishops or clerics we command that they be deposed; if religious or laics, that they be cut off from communion.

12. *Anna Comnena,* Alexiad: Trial of Basil the Bogomil (*1140s*)

Reprinted by permission of the publishers, Routledge & Kegan Paul Ltd., London, and Barnes & Noble, Inc., New York, from Anna Comnena, *The Alexiad of the Princess Anna Comnena,* trans. Elizabeth A. S. Dawes (London: Kegan Paul, Trench, Trubner & Co., Ltd., 1928), pp. 412–14, 415–18.

After this, in the course of the years of his reign, a very great cloud of heretics arose, and the nature of their heresy was new and hitherto quite unknown to the church. For two very evil and worthless doctrines which had been known in former times, now coalesced; the impiety, as it might be called, of the Manichæans, which we also call the Paulician heresy, and the shamelessness of the Massalians. This was the doctrine of the Bogomils compounded of the Massalians and the Manichæans. And probably it existed even before my father's time, but in secret; for the sect of the Bogomils is very clever in aping virtue. And you would not find any long-haired worldling belonging to the Bogomils, for their wickedness was hidden under the cloak and cowl. A Bogomil looks gloomy and is covered up to the nose and walks with a stoop and mutters, but within he is an uncontrollable wolf. And this most pernicious race, which was like a snake hiding in a hole, my father lured and brought out to the light by chanting mysterious spells. For now that he had rid himself of much of his anxiety about the East and the West he turned his attention to more spiritual matters. For in all things he was superior to other men; in teaching he surpassed those whose profession was teaching; in battles and strategy he excelled those who were admired for their exploits. By this time the fame of the Bogomils had spread everywhere. (For Basil, a monk, was very wily in handling the impiety of the Bogomils; he had twelve disciples whom he called "apostles," and also dragged about with him some female disciples, wretched women of loose habits and thoroughly bad, and he disseminated his wickedness everywhere.) This evil attacked many souls like fire, and the Emperor's soul could not brook it, so he began investigating the heresy. He had some of the Bogomils brought to the palace and all proclaimed a certain Basil as the teacher and chief representative of the Bogomilian heresy. Of these, one Diblatius was kept in prison, and as he would not confess when questioned, he was subjected to torture and then informed against the man called Basil, and the disciples he had chosen. Accordingly the Emperor entrusted several men with the search for him. And Satanael's arch-satrap, Basil, was brought to light, in monk's habit, with a withered countenance, clean shaven and tall of stature. The Emperor, wishing to elicit his inmost thoughts by compulsion under the disguise of persuasion, at once invited the man on some righteous pretext. And he even rose from his chair to greet him, and made him sit by him and share his table, and threw out his whole fishing-line and fixed various baits on the hooks for this voracious whale to devour. And he made this monk, who was so many-sided in wickedness, swallow all the poison he offered him by pretending that he wished to become his disciple, and not he only, but probably his brother, the Sebastocrator Isaac, also; he pretended too to value all the words he spoke as if they came from a divine voice and to defer to him in all things, provided only that the villain Basil would effect his soul's salvation. "Most reverend father," he would say (for the Emperor rubbed sweets on the rim of the cup so that this demoniac should vomit forth his black thoughts), "I admire thee for thy virtue, and beseech thee to teach me the new doctrines thy Reverence has introduced, as those of our Churches are practically worthless and do not bring anybody to virtue." But the monk at first put on airs and he, that was really an ass, dragged about the lion's skin with him everywhere and shied at the Emperor's words, and yet was puffed up with his praises, for the Emperor even had him at his table. And in all this the Emperor's cousin [?] the Sebastocrator aided and abetted him in the play; and finally Basil spued out the dogmas of his heresy. And how was this done? A curtain divided the women's apartments from the room where the two Emperors sat with the wretch who blurted out and openly declared all he had in his soul; whilst a secretary sitting on the inner side of the curtain committed his words to writing. And the nonsense-monger seemed to be the teacher while the Emperor pretended to be the pupil, and the secretary wrote down his doctrines. And that man, stricken of God, spun together all that horrible stuff and did not shun any abominable dogma, but even despised our theology and misrepresented all our ecclesiastical administration. And as for the churches, woe is me! he called our sacred churches the temples of devils, and our consecration of the body and blood of our one and greatest High Priest and Victim he considered and condemned as worthless. And what followed? the Emperor threw off his disguise and drew the curtain aside; and the whole senate was gathered together and the military contingent mustered, and the elders of the church were present too. The episcopal throne of the Queen of Cities was at that time occupied by that most blessed of patriarchs, Lord Nicholas, the Grammarian. Then the execrable doctrines were read out, and proof was impossible to attack. And the defendant did not deny anything, but immediately bared his head and proceeded to counter-demonstrations and professed himself willing to undergo fire, scourging and a thousand deaths. For these erring Bogomils believe that they can bear any suffering without feeling pain, as the angels forsooth will pluck them out of the fire. And although all . . . reproached him for his impiety, even those whom he had involved in his own ruin, he remained the same Basil, an inflexible and very brave Bogomil. And although he was threatened with burning and other tortures he clung fast to his demon and embraced his Satanael. After he was consigned to prison the Emperor frequently sent for him and frequently exhorted him to forswear his impiety, but all the Emperor's exhortations left him unchanged. . . .

The Emperor had summoned Basil's disciples and fellow-mystics from all over the world, especially the so-called twelve disciples and made trial of their opinions, and found that they were openly Basil's followers. For the evil had gone deep even into very great houses and had affected a very large number. Consequently he condemned those aliens to be burnt, the leader of the chorus and the chorus too. When the Bogomils who had been discovered were assembled, some clung to their heresy, while others recanted absolutely and resisted their accusers strongly and expressed their abhorrence of the Bogomilian heresy. The Emperor was not inclined to believe them, and to prevent many a Christian being confounded with the Bogomils as being a Bogomil, and a Bogomil escaping as a Christian, he invented a new device for revealing clearly those who were really Christians. Accordingly the next day he took his seat on the imperial throne and many of the senate and the holy Synod were present and a chosen few of the monks who were learned men. Then all the Bogomils accused of heresy were placed together in the centre and the Emperor commanded each to be examined again. Some confessed to being Bogomils and adhered stoutly to their heresy, while others denied it absolutely and called themselves Christians and when accused by others did not yield an inch, so he glowered at them and said, "To-day two pyres shall be lighted and on one of them a cross shall be fixed in the ground itself. Then you shall all be given your choice and those who are ready to die to-day for their Christian faith, can separate themselves from the others and walk to the pyre with the cross, while those who cling to the Bogomilian heresy shall be thrown on the other. For it is better that even Christians should die, than live to be persecuted as Bogomils and offend the consciences of many. Go now and let each one of you choose his station." With this verdict against the Bogomils the Emperor pretended to have closed the matter. They were at once taken and led away and a large crowd had gathered and stood round about them. Then pyres were lighted, "seven times as large as they were wont to be," as the hymn-writer says, in the place called Tzycanisterin; the flames rose to the heavens, and the cross stood above the one; each of the condemned was given his choice to walk to which of the two pyres he wished, as all were destined to be burnt. Seeing that there was no escape, the orthodox among them walked to the pyre with the cross, ready really to suffer martyrdom; whereas the godless ones who clung to their abominable heresy turned to the other. And they were all on the point of being thrown on the pyres at the same time and the bystanders all grieved for the Christians who were now to be burnt, and were very wroth against the Emperor, for they were ignorant of his plan. But an order from the Emperor came just in time to prevent the executioners carrying out their duties. Having in this way obtained certain proof of those who were really Bogomils, he released the Christians, who had been falsely accused, with many admonitions. The others he recommitted to prison, but had the impious Basil's apostles separated from the rest. And these he sent for daily, and taught some himself, exhorting them earnestly to abandon their hideous religion, and for the others he ordered some picked men of the hierarchy to come every day and teach them the orthodox faith and advise them to relinquish the Bogomilian heresy. And some of them did change for the better and were released from confinement, but others were kept in prison and died in their heresy, but were amply supplied with food and clothing.

However all the members of the holy synod and the chief monks, as well as the patriarch of that time, Nicholas, decreed that Basil who was the heresiarch and quite unrepentant, deserved to be burnt. The Emperor was of the same opinion and after conversing with him several times and recognizing that the man was mischievous and would not abandon his heresy, he finally had an immense pyre built in the Hippodrome. A very large trench was dug and a quantity of wood, all tall trees piled up together, made the structure look like a mountain. When the pile was lighted, a great crowd slowly collected on the floor and steps of the circus in eager expectation of what was to happen. On the opposite side a cross was fixed and the impious man was given a choice, for if he dreaded the fire and changed his mind, and walked to the cross, then he should be delivered from burning. A number of heretics were there watching their leader Basil. He shewed himself contemptuous of all punishment and threats, and while he was still at a distance from the fire he began to laugh and talk marvels, saying that angels would snatch him from the middle of the fire, and he proceeded to chant these words of David's, "It shall not come nigh thee; only with thine eyes shalt thou behold." But when the crowd stood aside and allowed him to have a free view of that terrifying sight, the burning pyre (for even at a good distance he could feel the fire, and saw the flames rising high and as it were thundering and shooting out sparks of fire which rose to the top of the stone obelisk which stands in the centre of the Hippodrome), then the bold fellow seemed to flinch from the fire and be disturbed. For as if wholly desperate, he constantly turned away his eyes and clapped his hands and beat his thigh. And yet in spite of being thus affected by the mere sight he was adamant. For the fire did not soften his iron will, nor did the messages sent by the Emperor subdue him. For either great madness had seized him under the present stress of misfortunes and he had lost his mind and had no power to decide about what was advantageous; or, as seems more likely, the devil that possessed his soul had steeped it in the deepest darkness. So there stood that abominable Basil, unmoved by any threat or fear, and gaped now at the fire and now at the bystanders. And all thought him quite mad for he did not rush to the pyre nor did he draw back, but stood fixed and immovable on the spot he had first taken up. Now many tales were going round and his marvellous talk was bandied about on every tongue, so the executioners were afraid that the demons protecting Basil might perhaps, by God's permission, work some wonderful new miracle, and the wretch be seen snatched unharmed from the middle of the mighty fire and transported to some very frequented place. In that case the second state would be worse than the first, so they decided to make an experiment. For, while he was talking marvels and boasting that he would be seen unharmed in the middle of the fire, they took his cloak and said, "Now let us see whether the fire will touch your garments," and they threw it right into the middle of the pyre. But Basil was so uplifted by the demon that was deluding him that he said, "Look at my cloak floating up to the sky!" Then they, "recognizing the web from the edge," took him and pushed him, clothes, shoes and all, into the middle of the pyre. And the flames, as if deeply enraged against him, ate the impious man up, without any odour arising or even a fresh appearance of smoke, only one thin smoky line could be seen in the midst of the flames. For even the elements are excited against the impious; whereas, to speak truthfully, they spare those beloved of God, just as once upon a time in Babylon the fire retreated from those young men who were dear to God, and enclosed them like a golden chamber. In this case the men who lifted up the accursed Basil had scarcely placed him on the pyre before the flames seemed to dart forward to snatch hold of him. Then the people looking on clamoured loudly and demanded that all the rest who belonged to Basil's pernicious sect should be thrown into the fire as well, but the Emperor did not allow it but ordered them to be confined in the porches and verandahs of the largest palace. After this the concourse was dismissed. Later, the godless ones were transferred to another very strong prison into which they were cast and after pining away for a long time died in their impiety. This was the last and crowning act of the Emperor's long labours and successes and it was an innovation of startling boldness.

B. The Quest for Holiness

13. *Athanasius,* Life of St. Antony

Athanasius, *Life of Antony,* trans. H. Ellershaw and Archibald Robertson, A Select Library of Nicene and Post-Nicene Fathers of the Christian Church, Second Series, Vol. IV (New York: The Christian Literature Company, 1892), 195–96, 199–200, 209–10, 219–20.

Antony you must know was by descent an Egyptian: his parents were of good family and possessed considerable wealth, and as they were Christians he also was reared in the same Faith. In infancy he was brought up with his parents, knowing nought else but them and his home. But when he was grown and arrived at boyhood, and was advancing in years, he could not endure to learn letters, not caring to associate with other boys; but all his desire was, as it is written of Jacob, to live a plain man at home. With his parents he used to attend the Lord's House, and neither as a child was he idle nor when older did he despise them; but was both obedient to his father and mother and attentive to what was read, keeping in his heart what was profitable in what he heard. And though as a child brought up in moderate affluence, he did not trouble his parents for varied or luxurious fare, nor was this a source of pleasure to him; but was content simply with what he found nor sought anything further.

After the death of his father and mother he was left alone with one little sister: his age was about eighteen or twenty, and on him the care both of home and sister rested. Now it was not six months after the death of his parents, and going according to custom into the Lord's House, he communed with himself and reflected as he walked how the Apostles left all and followed the Saviour; and how they in the Acts sold their possessions and brought and laid them at the Apostles' feet for distribution to the needy, and what and how great a hope was laid up for them in heaven. Pondering over these things he entered the church, and it happened the Gospel was being read, and he heard the Lord saying to the rich man, "If thou wouldest be perfect, go and sell that thou hast and give to the poor; and come follow Me and thou shalt have treasure in heaven." Antony, as though God had put him in mind of the Saints, and the passage had been read on his account, went out immediately from the church, and gave the possessions of his forefathers to the villagers—they were three hundred acres, productive and very fair—that they should be no more a clog upon himself and his sister. And all the rest that was movable he sold, and having got together much money he gave it to the poor, reserving a little however for his sister's sake.

And again as he went into the church, hearing the Lord say in the Gospel, "be not anxious for the morrow," he could stay no longer, but went out and gave those things also to the poor. Having committed his sister to known and faithful virgins, and put her into a convent to be brought up, he henceforth devoted himself outside his house to discipline, taking heed to himself and training himself with patience. For there were not yet so many monasteries in Egypt, and no monk at all knew of the distant desert; but all who wished to give heed to themselves practised the discipline in solitude near their own village. . . .

More and more confirmed in his purpose, he hurried to the mountain, and having found a fort, so long deserted that it was full of creeping things, on the other side of the river; he crossed over to it and dwelt there. The reptiles, as though some one were chasing them, immediately left the place. But he built up the entrance completely, having stored up loaves for six months—this is a custom of the Thebans, and the loaves often remain fresh a whole year—and as he found water within, he descended as into a shrine, and abode within by himself, never going forth nor looking at any one who came. Thus he employed a long time training himself, and received loaves, let down from above, twice in the year.

But those of his acquaintances who came, since he did not permit them to enter, often used to spend days and nights outside, and heard as it were crowds within clamouring, dinning, sending forth piteous voices and crying, "Go from what is ours. What dost thou even in the desert? Thou canst not abide our attack." So at first those outside thought there were some men fighting with him, and that they had entered by ladders; but when stooping down they saw through a hole there was nobody, they were afraid, accounting them to be demons, and they called on Antony. Them he quickly heard, though he had not given a thought to the demons, and coming to the door he besought them to depart and not to be afraid, "for thus," said he, "the demons make their seeming onslaughts against those who are cowardly. Sign yourselves therefore with the cross, and depart boldly, and let these make sport for themselves." So they departed fortified with the sign of the Cross. But he remained in no wise harmed by the evil spirits, nor was he wearied with the contest, for there came to his aid visions from above, and the weakness of the foe relieved him of much trouble and armed him with greater zeal. For his acquaintances used often to come expecting to find him dead, and would hear him singing, "Let God arise and let His enemies be scattered, let them also that hate Him flee before His face. As smoke vanisheth, let them vanish; as wax melteth before the face of fire, so let the sinners perish from the face of God"; and again, "All nations compassed me about, and in the name of the Lord I requited them."

And so for nearly twenty years he continued training himself in solitude, never going forth, and but seldom seen by any. After this, when many were eager and wishful to imitate his discipline, and his acquaintances came and began to cast down and wrench off the door by force, Antony, as from a shrine, came forth initiated in the mysteries and filled with the Spirit of God. Then for the first time he was seen outside the fort by those who came to see him. And they, when they saw him, wondered at the sight, for he had the same habit of body as before, and was neither fat, like a man without exercise, nor lean from fasting and striving with the demons, but he was just the same as they had known him before his retirement. And again his soul was free from blemish, for it was neither contracted as if by grief, nor relaxed by pleasure, nor possessed by laughter or dejection, for he was not troubled when he beheld the crowd, nor overjoyed at being saluted by so many. But he was altogether even as being guided by reason, and abiding in a natural state. Through him the Lord healed the bodily ailments of many present, and cleansed others from evil spirits. And He gave grace to Antony in speaking, so that he consoled many that were sorrowful, and set those at variance at one, exhorting all to prefer the love of Christ before all that is in the world. And while he exhorted and advised them to remember the good things to come, and the loving-kindness of God towards us, "Who spared not His own Son, but delivered Him up for us all," he persuaded many to embrace the solitary life. And thus it happened in the end that cells arose even in the mountains, and the desert was colonised by monks, who came forth from their own people, and enrolled themselves for the citizenship in the heavens. . . .

But when he saw himself beset by many, and not suffered to withdraw himself according to his intent as he wished, fearing because of the signs which the Lord wrought by him, that either he should be puffed up, or that some other should think of him above what he ought to think, he considered and set off to go into the upper Thebaid, among those to whom he was unknown. And having received loaves from the brethren, he sat down by the bank of the river, looking whether a boat would go by, that, having embarked thereon, he might go up the river with them. While he was considering these things, a voice came to him from above, "Antony, wither goest thou and wherefore?" But he no way disturbed, but as he had been accustomed to be called often thus, giving ear to it, answered, saying, "Since the multitude permit me not to be still, I wish to go into the upper Thebaid on account of the many hindrances that come upon me here, and especially because they demand of me things beyond my power." But the voice said unto him, "Even though you should go into the Thebaid, or even though, as you have in mind, you should go down to the Bucolia, you will have to endure more, aye, double the amount of toil. But if you wish really to be in quiet, depart now into the inner desert." And when Antony said, "Who will show me the way for I know it not?" immediately the voice pointed out to him Saracens about to go that way. So Antony approached, and drew near them, and asked that he might go with them into the desert. And they, as though they had been commanded by Providence, received him willingly. And having journeyed with them three days and three nights, he came to a very lofty mountain, and at the foot of the mountain ran a clear spring, whose waters were sweet and very cold; outside there was a plain and a few uncared-for palm trees.

Antony then, as it were, moved by God, loved the place, for this was the spot which he who had spoken with him by the banks of the river had pointed out. So having first received loaves from his fellow travellers, he abode in the mountain alone, no one else being with him. And recognising it as his own home, he remained in that place for the future. But the Saracens, having seen the earnestness of Antony, purposely used to journey that way, and joyfully brought him loaves, while now and then the palm trees also afforded him a poor and frugal relish. But after this, the brethren learning of the place, like children mindful of their father, took care to send to him. But when Antony saw that the bread was the cause of trouble and hardships to some of them, to spare the monks this, he resolved to ask some of those who came to bring him a spade, an axe, and a little corn. And when these were brought, he went over the land round the mountain, and having found a small plot of suitable ground, tilled it; and having a plentiful supply of water for watering, he sowed. This doing year by year, he got his bread from thence, rejoicing that thus he would be troublesome to no one, and because he kept himself from being a burden to anybody. But after this, seeing again that people came, he cultivated a few pot-herbs, that he who came to him might have some slight solace after the labour of that hard journey. At first, however, the wild beasts in the desert, coming because of the water, often injured his seeds and husbandry. But he, gently laying hold of one of them, said to them all, "Why do you hurt me, when I hurt none of you? Depart, and in the name of the Lord come not nigh this spot." And from that time forward, as though fearful of his command, they no more came near the place.

So he was alone in the inner mountain, spending his time in prayer and discipline. And the brethren who served him asked that they might come every month and bring him olives, pulse and oil, for by now he was an old man. There then he passed his life, and endured such great wrestlings, "Not against flesh and blood," as it is written, but against opposing demons, as we learned from those who visited him. For there they heard tumults, many voices, and, as it were, the clash of arms. At night they saw the mountain become full of wild beasts, and him also fighting as though against visible beings, and praying against them. And those who came to him he encouraged, while kneeling he contended and prayed to the Lord. Surely it was a marvellous thing that a man, alone in such a desert, feared neither the demons who rose up against him, nor the fierceness of the four-footed beasts and creeping things, for all they were so many. But in truth, as it is written, "He trusted in the Lord as Mount Sion," with a mind unshaken and undisturbed; so that the demons rather fled from him, and the wild beasts, as it is written, "kept peace with him." . . .

A few days after, as he was working (for he was careful to work hard), some one stood at the door and pulled the plait which he was working, for he used to weave baskets, which he gave to those who came in return for what they brought him. . . .

It is worth while that I should relate, and that you, as you wish it, should hear what his death was like. For this end of his is worthy of imitation. According to his custom he visited the monks in the outer mountain, and having learned from Providence that his own end was at hand, he said to the brethren, "This is my last visit to you which I shall make. And I shall be surprised if we see each other again in this life. At length the time of my departure is at hand, for I am near a hundred and five years old." And when they heard it they wept, and embraced, and kissed the old man. But he, as though sailing from a foreign city to his own, spoke joyously, and exhorted them "Not to grow idle in their labours, nor to become faint in their training, but to live as though dying daily. And as he had said before, zealously to guard the soul from foul thoughts, eagerly to imitate the Saints, and to have nought to do with the Meletian schismatics, for you know their wicked and profane character. Nor have any fellowship with the Arians, for their impiety is clear to all. Nor be disturbed if you see the judges protect them, for it shall cease, and their pomp is mortal and of short duration. Wherefore keep yourselves all the more untainted by them, and observe the traditions of the fathers, and chiefly the holy faith in our Lord Jesus Christ, which you have learned from the Scripture, and of which you have often been put in mind by me." . . .

But he, knowing the custom, and fearing that his body would be treated this way [i.e., divided into relics], hastened, and having bidden farewell to the monks in the outer mountain entered the inner mountain, where he was accustomed to abide. And after a few months he fell sick. Having summoned those who were there—they were two in number who had remained in the mountain fifteen years, practising the discipline and attending on Antony on account of his age. . . .

Having said this, when they had kissed him, he lifted up his feet, and as though he saw friends coming to him and was glad because of them—for as he lay his countenance appeared joyful—he died and was gathered to the fathers. And they afterward, according to his commandment, wrapped him up and buried him, hiding his body underground. And no one knows to this day where it was buried, save those two only. . . .

14. *Basil of Caesarea,* The Long Rules

Reprinted by permission of The Catholic University of America Press from M. Monica Wagner, trans., *Saint Basil: Ascetical Works,* Fathers of the Church, Vol. IX (New York: Fathers of the Church, Inc., 1950), 247–50, 289–91.

Q. 7. On the Necessity of Living in the Company of Those Who Are Striving for the Same Objective—That of Pleasing God—and the Difficulty and Hazards of Living as a Solitary.

Since your words have convinced us that it is dangerous to live in company with those who hold the commandments of God in light regard, we consider it logical to inquire whether one who retires from society should live in solitude or with brethren who are of the same mind and who have set before themselves the same goal, that is, the devout life.

R. I consider that life passed in company with a number of persons in the same habitation is more advantageous in many respects. My reasons are, first, that no one of us is self-sufficient as regards corporeal necessities, but we require one another's aid in supplying our needs. The foot, to cite an analogy, possesses one kind of power and lacks nother, and without the co-operation of the other members of the ody it finds itself incapable of carrying on its activity independently r any length of time, nor does it have wherewithal to supply what is cking. Similarly, in the solitary life, what is at hand becomes useless us and what is wanting cannot be provided, since God, the Creator, ecreed that we should require the help of one another, as it is written, that we might associate with one another. Again, apart from this onsideration, the doctrine of the charity of Christ does not permit he individual to be concerned solely with his own private interests. 'Charity," says the Apostle, "seeketh not her own." But a life passed n solitude is concerned only with the private service of individual needs. This is openly opposed to the law of love which the Apostle fulfilled, who sought not what was profitable to himself but to many that they might be saved. Furthermore, a person living in solitary retirement will not readily discern his own defects, since he has no one to dmonish and correct him with mildness and compassion. In fact, admonition even from an enemy often produces in a prudent man the desire for amendment. But the cure of sin is wrought with understanding by him who loves sincerely; for Holy Scripture says: "for he that loveth correcteth betimes." Such a one it is very difficult to find in a solitude, if in one's prior state of life one had not been associated with such a person. The solitary, consequently, experiences the truth of the saying, "Woe to him that is alone, for when he falleth he hath none to lift him up." Moreover, the majority of the commandments are easily observed by several persons living together, but not so in the case of one living alone; for, while he is obeying one commandment, the practice of another is being interfered with. For example, when he is visiting the sick, he cannot show hospitality to the stranger and, in the imparting and sharing of necessities (especially when the ministrations are prolonged), he is prevented from giving zealous attention to [other] tasks. As a result, the greatest commandment and the one especially conducive to salvation is not observed, since the hungry are not fed nor the naked clothed. Who, then, would choose this ineffectual and unprofitable life in preference to that which is both fruitful and in accordance with the Lord's command?

Besides, if all we who are united in the one hope of our calling are one body with Christ as our Head, we are also members, one of another. If we are not joined together by union in the Holy Spirit in the harmony of one body, but each of us should choose to live in solitude, we would not serve the common good in the ministry according to God's good pleasure, but would be satisfying our own passion for self-gratification. How could we, divided and separated, preserve the status and the mutual service of members or our subordinate relationship to our Head which is Christ? It is impossible, indeed, to rejoice with him who receives an honor or to sympathize with him who suffers when, by reason of their being separated from one another, each person cannot, in all likelihood, be kept informed about the affairs of his neighbor. In addition, since no one has the capacity to receive all spiritual gifts, but the grace of the Spirit is given proportionately to the faith of each, when one is living in association with others, the grace privately bestowed on each individual becomes the common possession of his fellows. "To one, indeed, is given the word of wisdom; and to another, the word of knowledge; to another, faith, to another, prophecy, to another, the grace of healing," and so on. He who receives any of these gifts does not possess it for his own sake but rather for the sake of others, so that, in the life passed in community, the operation of the Holy Spirit in the individual is at the same time necessarily transmitted to all. He who lives alone, consequently, and has, perhaps, one gift renders it ineffectual by leaving it in disuse, since it lies buried within him. How much danger there is in this all of you know who have read the Gospel. On the other hand, in the case of several persons living together, each enjoys his own gift and enhances it by giving others a share, besides reaping benefit from the gifts of others as if they were his own.

Q. 28. What the Attitude of All Should Be Toward the Disobedient.

R. All should certainly be compassionate at first toward one who obeys the Lord's commands reluctantly, as toward an ailing member of their body. The superior, also, should endeavor by private exhortation to cure his weakness; but, if he persists in disobedience and is not amenable to correction, he should be severely reprimanded in the presence of the whole community and a remedy, together with every form of exhortation, should be administered. If he is neither converted after much admonition nor cures himself by his own actions with tears and lamentations, being, as the proverb has it, "his own destroyer," we should, as physicians do, cut him off from the body of the brethren as a corrupt and wholly useless member. . . .

In general, then, whoever refuses the remedy applied by the superior acts inconsistently even with himself; for, if he does not take kindly to being governed and his own will acts as his arbiter, why does he continue to live under a superior? Why does he take him as the director of his life? But, having allowed himself, once and for all, to be reckoned with the body of the community, if he has been judged a suitable vessel for the ministry, when a command appears to be beyond his strength, leaving the decision regarding this to the one who imposed the command, he should show himself obedient and submissive even unto death, remembering that the Lord became "obedient unto death, even to the death of the cross." To rebel and to contradict, however, are indications of many evils: a weak faith, a doubtful hope, and a self-important and arrogant character. His disobedience, indeed, implies that he holds in contempt him who gave the order. On the other hand, one who trusts in the promises of God and keeps his hope fixed on these will never draw back from commands, however difficult to execute they may be, knowing that the sufferings of this time are not worthy to be compared with the future glory to be revealed. Furthermore, one who is convinced that "he that humbleth himself shall be exalted" and bears in mind that "that which is at present momentary and light of our tribulation worketh above measure exceedingly an eternal weight of glory," obeys with greater alacrity than he who gives the order expects. . . .

Part Three

THE BYZANTINE COUNTRYSIDE

Like other ancient and medieval states, the Byzantine Empire depended on agriculture. The condition of the peasantry was fundamental to the social structure of the empire. The characteristic form of early Byzantine agricultural organization was the great estate, worked by hundreds of sharecroppers. To prevent these *coloni* from fleeing, Diocletian and his successors bound them to the soil and required the return of runaways. These regulations were incorporated in the legal code compiled by Theodosius II (408–450) (Reading No. 15). This bondage of most peasants continued through the age of Justinian (527–565) (Reading No. 16).

With the great Persian and Arabic invasions of the early seventh century, a new era seemingly dawned for *coloni* in Asia Minor, the principal remaining region of the empire. As the invaders devastated them, the great estates broke up, and in their place appeared villages of free peasants. Some of them certainly owed military service to the state in return for their lands. The village as a unit owned the uncultivated part of its district, and paid a lump sum of taxes; land under the plow was privately owned and individually cultivated, unlike the situation in medieval Western Europe. Our chief evidence concerning the free peasantry comes from the Farmer's Law, dated in the late seventh or early eighth centuries, and here given in its entirety (Reading No. 17).

During the ninth and tenth centuries, peace returned to Asia Minor; generals, bureaucrats, and even fortunate peasants invested in land, created great estates, and founded such families as Phocas, Sclerus, and Comnenus. Taking advantage of moments of scarcity, a wealthy man might make loans to a peasant who pledged his land as security; if the debtor could not repay, his land fell to the lender, and he became a sharecropper. Once a great landowner had thus gained a foothold in the midst of a free village, its other inhabitants could be pressured into selling their property to him. The emperors of the tenth century recognized that the disappearance of the free peasantry threatened the military and financial strength of the empire, while the rise of powerful landlords created a challenge to the Macedonian Dynasty (867–1057) itself.

In actuality a usurper, Romanus I Lecapenus (919–944), a peasant's son who had made himself co-emperor with Constantine VII, first recognized the danger and inaugurated a series of laws to protect the poor (*ptochoi* or *penetes*) from the powerful (*dynatoi*). His first law, in 922, established classes of individuals who had the right of preference (*protimesis*) in purchasing if a villager was compelled to sell land; his fellow taxpayers, members of the same village, enjoyed priority over any outsider (i.e., wealthy landlord). The stratagems to which the powerful resorted are clearly stated in this law (Reading No. 18). A severe famine in the winter of 927–928 compelled many peasants to sell their property, which the wealthy bought at a fraction of the true values. In 934 Romanus published a second land law which rigorously forbade the powerful to buy land from the poor and commanded the expulsion of those who had done so. The poor, however, had to repay within three years the purchase price for all legally valid sales, and pay for or restore improvements made by the wealthy buyer (Reading No. 19). These laws were renewed by Constantine VII (945–959) and Romanus II (959–963); soldier's property also was declared inalienable.

Romanus II was succeeded by his two young sons, Basil II (963–1025) and Constantine VIII (963–1028). To protect the throne, their mother married the prominent general Nicephorus Phocas, who ruled as co-emperor Nicephorus II (963–969). Sprung from a prominent landowning family, Nicephorus had little sympathy with the free peasantry. His law regarding alienations complained of the injustice done the rich by previous legislation (for the rules on legal preference had applied equally to rich and poor) ; in the name of equity, he permitted only sales among members of the same social class. This has usually been understood as a covert sanction for acquisitions by the powerful, perhaps made through third parties (Reading No. 20). But as a general, Nicephorus II was eager to maintain the army, so another law restricted alienations by soldier-peasants and raised the minimum value of a military holding; only if the soldier owned land worth more than twelve pounds of gold was he free to sell (Reading No. 21).

In 996, Basil II, now senior emperor, published a massive ordinance, many sections of which bear on the peasant and his lands. The tone of the law is intensely personal, and added to it are marginal notes apparently written by Basil himself. After a description of the evils inflicted by the powerful, including the upstart peasant Philocales, the emperor declares that all lands unjustly purchased since 934 must be restored; no period of wrongful possession will justify such acquisitions. Regulations concerning country fairs throw a ray of light into the obscure life of the peasants (Reading No. 22). While Basil II rigorously enforced his land laws, such successors as Constantine IX Monomachus allowed them to lapse, and the aristocracy quickly gained the upper hand. After 1025, the peasants were again reduced to sharecropping on great estates, and the army of land-owning soldiers was replaced by a mercenary force. From the ruin of the free peasantry came the decay of the Byzantine state.

A. The Colonus

15. *Theodosian Code*

Theodosian Code, Titles 5.17.1–2, and 5.18.1–5. Reprinted by permission of the publisher and the translator Clyde Pharr from *The Theodosian Code and Novels and the Sirmondian Constitutions* (Princeton, N. J.: Princeton University Press, 1952). Copyright © 1952 by Clyde Pharr. The extracts are from pp. 115–16.

TITLE 17: FUGITIVE COLONI, INQUILINI, AND SLAVES (DE FUGITIVIS COLONIS, INQUILINIS ET SERVIS).

1. Emperor Constantine Augustus to the Provincials.

Any person in whose possession a colonus that belongs to another is found not only shall restore the aforesaid colonus to his birth status but also shall assume the capitation tax for this man for the time that he was with him.

1. Coloni also who meditate flight must be bound with chains and reduced to a servile condition, so that by virtue of their condemnation to slavery, they shall be compelled to fulfill the duties that befit freemen.

Given on the third day before the kalends of November in the year of the consulship of Pacatianus and Hilarianus.—October 30, 332.

2. Emperors Gratian, Valentinian, and Theodosius Augustuses to Cynegius, Praetorian Prefect.

If any person through solicitation should receive a colonus belonging to another or by concealment should harbor him, he shall be compelled to pay six ounces of gold for him if he is a colonus belonging to a private person, and a pound of gold if he is a colonus belonging to an imperial patrimonial estate.

Given on the eighth day before the kalends of November at Constantinople in the year of the consulship of Emperor Designate Honorius and of Evodius.—October 25, 386. . . .

TITLE 18: INQUILINI AND COLONI (DE INQUILINIS ET COLONIS).

1. Emperors Honorius and Theodosius Augustuses to Palladius, Praetorian Prefect.

If a person who is a colonus or inquilinus by birth status has departed from a landholding thirty years before and if, through a continuous period of silence, he has not been brought back to his native soil, every unfounded action against him or the person who perchance now possesses him shall be completely excluded. It is Our will that this same number of years shall be observed likewise for future times.

1. But if within this period of thirty years any colonus by birth status has departed from a landholding, whether he escaped through flight or was abducted by his own wish or through solicitation, and if there should be no doubt concerning his status, We order that all controversy shall be removed and that he, together with his family, shall be restored without delay to the status to which he was born.

2. But if perchance the man whose ownership is contested should be

destroyed by the lot of fate, We command that, with swift execution of the order, his offspring shall be recalled to the legal claims of the fields, along with all their peculia and wages, just as though the man who had died were surviving.

3. In the case of women, to be sure, it is Our will that there shall be a different regulation. Thus if women who are proved to be colonae by birth status have departed twenty years before from the land to which they were obligated, all right of recovery shall cease. But We do not permit the owners to lose their right to recover those women who are proved to have departed within the aforementioned period of time and concerning whose status there is no doubt. However, this condition shall be observed, namely, that a substitute woman shall not be refused, together with a third part of the offspring of the fugitive colona, that have been begotten by a colonus belonging to another, provided that substitutes for the children may also be furnished. 4. But if such woman did not settle upon another person's landed estate, but obtained a union with a man who is free and legally independent, with the intention of living in the city or in any other district, and if her return is demanded within the specified time, in accordance with the ancient constitutions, all her progeny shall be recovered. 5. Moreover, We decree that in the case of persons that seek recovery, their suits when once attested shall be valid, provided that they prove that they have formally instituted an action.

Given on the sixth day before the kalends of July at Ravenna in the year of the consulship of Monaxius and Plinta.—June 26, 419.

16. *Deed of Surety for a Serf (A.D. 579)*

Reprinted by permission of the publisher from the Loeb Classical Library, A. S. Hunt and C. C. Edgar, eds. and trans., *Select Papyri: Non-Literary Papyri* (Cambridge, Mass.: Harvard University Press, 1932), I, 77–81.

In the 4th year of the reign of our most godlike and pious master and greatest benefactor Flavius Tiberius Constantinus the eternal Augustus and Imperator, Phamenoth 25, 12th indiction. To the most magnificent heirs of Apion of glorious memory, patrician, landowners in this illustrious city of Oxyrhynchus, through their servant Menas who is acting on their behalf and assuming for his masters, the said all-honoured persons, the rights and obligations of the agreement, from Aurelius Pamouthius, lead-worker, son of George and Anniana, of the city of Oxyrhynchus. I acknowledge of my free will, swearing the divine and imperial oath, that I accept from your magnificence, through your representatives, the charge of and responsibility for Aurelius Abraham son of Herminus and Herais, who comes from the estate of Great Tarouthinas belonging to your magnificence in the Oxyrhynchite nome and is enrolled as your farmer, engaging that he shall uninterruptedly remain and abide on his proper estate along with his family and wife and animals and all his household gear, I being answerable for all that regards his person or his status as your bondsman, and that he shall in no wise leave the said estate or remove to another place; and if he is required of me by your magnificence through your representatives at any date and for any reason whatsoever, I will bring and deliver him in a public place debarred from every sanctuary and subterfuge, even where I received him, in the guard-room of your said honourable house. If I fail to do this, I agree to pay down for his desertion and my failure to deliver him 8 gold solidi, to be really and truly exacted. This deed of surety, made in a single copy, is valid, and in answer to the formal question I have given my assent. (Subscribed) Executed by me, Anastasius. (Endorsed) Deed of surety of Pamouthius, lead-worker, son of George, of Oxyrhynchus, accepting responsibility for Abraham son of Herminus of the estate of Tarouthinas.

B. The Free Peasant

17. *The Farmer's Law (seventh–eighth centuries)*

"The Farmer's Law," trans. W. Ashburner. Reprinted by permission of the Council of the Hellenic Society from *Journal of Hellenic Studies,* XXXII (1912), 87–95.

Chapters of the Farmers Law by Way of Extract from the Volume of Justinian.

1. The farmer who is working his own field must be just and must not encroach on his neighbour's furrows. If a farmer persists in encroaching and docks a neighbouring lot—if he did this in ploughing-time, he loses his ploughing; if it was in sowing-time that he made this encroachment, he loses his seed and his husbandry and his crop—the farmer who encroached.

2. If a farmer without the landowner's cognizance enters and ploughs or sows, let him not receive either wages for his ploughing or the crop for his sowing—no, not even the seed that has been cast.

3. If two farmers agree one with the other before two or three witnesses to exchange lands and they agreed for all time, let their determination and their exchange remain firm and secure and unassailable.

4. If two farmers, *A* and *B*, agree to exchange their lands for the season of sowing and *A* draws back, then, if the seed was cast, they may not draw back; but if the seed was not cast they may draw back; but if *A* did not plough while *B* did, *A* also shall plough.

5. If two farmers exchange lands either for a season or for all time, and one plot is found deficient as compared with the other, and this was not their agreement, let him who has more give an equivalent in land to him who has less; but if this was their agreement, let them give nothing in addition.

6. If a farmer who has a claim on a field enters against the sower's will and reaps, then, if he had a just claim, let him take nothing from it; but if his claim was baseless, let him provide twice over the crops that were reaped.

7. If two territories contend about a boundary or a field, let the judges consider it and they shall decide in favour of the territory which had the longer possession; but if there is an ancient landmark, let the ancient determination remain unassailed.

8. If a division wronged people in their lots or lands, let them have licence to undo the division.

9. If a farmer on shares reaps without the grantor's consent and robs him of his sheaves, as a thief shall he be deprived of all his crop.

10. A shareholder's portion is nine bundles, the grantor's one: he who divides outside these limits is accursed.

11. If a man takes land from an indigent farmer and agrees to plough only and to divide, let their agreement prevail; if they also agreed on sowing, let it prevail according to their agreement.

12. If a farmer takes from some indigent farmer his vineyard to work on a half-share and does not prune it as is fitting and dig it and fence it and dig it over, let him receive nothing from the produce.

13. If a farmer takes land to sow on a half-share, and when the season requires it does not plough but throws the seed on the surface, let him receive nothing from the produce because he played false and mocked the landowner.

14. If he who takes on a half-share the field of an indigent farmer who is abroad changes his mind and does not work the field, let him restore the produce twice over.

15. If he who takes on a half-share changes his mind before the season of working and gives notice to the landowner that he has not the strength and the landowner pays no attention, let the man who took on a half-share go harmless.

16. If a farmer takes over the farming of a vineyard or piece of land and agrees with the owner and takes earnest-money and starts and then draws back and gives it up, let him give the just value of the field and let the owner have the field.

17. If a farmer enters and works another farmer's woodland, for three years he shall take its profits for himself and then give the land back again to its owner.

18. If a farmer who is too poor to work his own vineyard takes flight and goes abroad, let those from whom claims are made by the public treasury gather in the grapes, and the farmer if he returns shall not be entitled to mulct them in the wine.

19. If a farmer who runs away from his own field pays every year the extraordinary taxes of the public treasury, let those who gather in the grapes and occupy the field be mulcted twofold.

20. If a man cuts another's wood without its owner's cognizance and works and sows it, let him have nothing from the produce.

21. If a farmer builds a house or plants a vineyard in another's field or plot and after a time there come the owners of the plot, they are not entitled to pull down the house or root up the vines, but they may take an equivalent in land. If the man who built or planted on the field that was not his own stoutly refuses to give an equivalent, the

owner of the plot is entitled to pull up the vines and pull down the house.

22. If a farmer at digging-time steals a spade or a hoe, and is afterwards recognized, let him pay its daily hire twelve folles; the same rule applies to him who steals a pruning-knife at pruning-time, or a scythe at reaping-time, or an axe at wood-cutting time.

Concerning Herdsmen.

23. If a neatherd in the morning receives an ox from a farmer and mixes it with the herd, and it happens that the ox is destroyed by a wolf, let him explain the accident to its master and he himself shall go harmless.

24. If a herdsmen who has received an ox loses it and on the same day on which the ox was lost does not give notice to the master of the ox that "I kept sight of the ox up to this or that point, but what is become of it I do not know," let him not go harmless, but, if he gave notice, let him go harmless.

25. If a herdsman receives an ox from a farmer in the morning and goes off and the ox gets separated from the mass of oxen and goes off and goes into cultivated plots or vineyards and does harm, let him not lose his wages, but let him make good the harm done.

26. If a herdsman in the morning receives an ox from a farmer and the ox disappears, let him swear in the Lord's name that he has not himself played foul and that he had no part in the loss of the ox and let him go harmless.

27. If a herdsman in the morning receives an ox from a farmer and it happens that it is wounded or blinded, let the herdsman swear that he has not himself played foul and let him go harmless.

28. If a herdsman on occasion of the loss of an ox or its wounding or blinding makes oath and is afterwards by good evidence proved a perjurer, let his tongue be cut out and let him make good the damage to the owner of the ox.

29. If a herdsman with the stick which he carries injures and wounds an ox or blinds it, he does not go scatheless and let him pay a penalty; but if he did it with a stone he goes scatheless.

30. If a man cuts a bell from an ox or a sheep and is recognized as

the thief, let him be whipped; and if the animal disappears, let him make it good who stole the bell.

31. If a tree stands on a lot, if the neighbouring lot is a garden and is overshadowed by the tree, the owner of the garden may trim its branches; but if there is no garden, the branches are not to be trimmed.

32. If a tree is cultivated by some one in an undivided place, and afterwards an allotment took place and it fell to another in his lot, let no one have possession of the tree but him who cultivated it; but if the owner of the place complains "I am injured by the tree," let them give instead of the tree another tree to the man who cultivated it and let them keep it.

33. If a guardian of fruit is found stealing in the place which he guards, let him lose his wages and be well beaten.

34. If a hired shepherd is found milking his flock without the owner's knowledge and selling them, let him be beaten and lose his wages.

35. If a man is found stealing another's straw, he shall restore it twice over.

36. If a man takes an ox or an ass or any beast without its owner's knowledge and goes off on business, let him give its hire twice over; and if it dies on the road, he shall give two for one, whatever it may be.

37. If a man takes an ox to work with and it dies, let the judges consider, and if it died in the very work for which he sought it, let him go harmless; but if it died in another work, he shall give the value of the ox.

38. If a man finds an ox doing harm in a vineyard or in a field or in another place, and does not give it back to its owner, on the terms of recovering from him all the destruction of his crops, but kills or wounds it, let him give ox for ox, ass for ass, or sheep for sheep.

39. If a man is cutting a branch in a thicket and does not pay attention, but it falls and kills an ox or an ass or anything else, he shall give soul for soul.

40. If a man is cutting a tree and unwittingly drops his axe from above and slays another's beast, he shall give it.

41. If a man steals an ox or an ass and is convicted, he shall be whipped and give it twice over and all its gain.

42. If while a man is trying to steal one ox from a herd, the herd is put to flight and eaten by wild beasts, let him be blinded.

43. If a man goes out to bring in his own ox or his ass, and in pursuing it pursues another with it, and does not bring it in also with him, but it is lost or eaten by wolves, let him give for an equivalent to its master an ox or an ass. But if he gave full notice and pointed out the place and showed in his defence that he could not get hold of it, let him go harmless.

44. If a man finds an ox in a wood and kills it, and takes the carcase let his hand be cut off.

45. If a slave kills one ox or ass or ram in a wood, his master shall make it good.

46. If a slave, while trying to steal by night, drives the sheep away from the flock in chasing them out of the fold, and they are lost or eaten by wild beasts, let him be hanged as a murderer.

47. If a man's slave often steals beasts at night, or often drives away flocks, his master shall make good what is lost on the ground that he knew his slave's guilt, but let the slave himself be hanged.

48. If a man finds an ox doing harm and does not give it to its master on being paid for the damage done, but cuts its ear or blinds it or cuts its tail, its master does not take it but takes another in its place.

49. If a man finds a pig doing harm or a sheep or a dog, he shall deliver it in the first place to its master; when he has delivered it a second time, he shall give notice to its master; the third time he may cut its tail or its ear or shoot it without incurring liability.

50. If an ox or an ass in trying to enter a vineyard or a garden falls into the ditch of the vineyard or of the garden and is killed, let the owner of the vineyard or garden go harmless.

51. If an ox or an ass in trying to enter a vineyard or a garden is spitted on the stakes of the fence, let the owner of the garden go harmless.

52. If a man sets a snare at harvest-time and a dog or a pig falls into it and die, let its owner go harmless.

53. If a man, after a first and second payment of damage, kills the animal which has done the damage instead of delivering it to its owner in order that he may recover the damage it has done, let him give what he killed.

54. If a man shuts up a pig or a dog and destroys it, he shall restore it twice over.

55. If a man kills a sheepdog and does not make confession but

there is an inroad of wild beasts into the sheepfold, and afterwards he who killed the dog is recognized, let him give the whole flock of sheep together with the value of the dog.

56. If a man lights a fire in his own wood or in his field and it happens that the fire spreads and burns houses or cultivated fields, he is not condemned unless he did it in a strong wind.

57. He who burns another's hillside or cuts another's trees is condemned in twice the damage.

58. Let him who burns the fence of a vineyard be beaten and have his hand branded and let him also pay twice the damage done.

59. Let him who cuts another's vines when they are in fruit or who roots them up have his hand cut off and pay the damage.

60. Let those who in harvest-time come into another man's furrow and cut bundles or ears of corn or pulse be whipped and stripped of their shirts.

61. Where people enter another man's vineyard or figyard, if they come to eat, let them go scatheless; if they are there to steal, let them be beaten and stripped of their shirts.

62. Let those who steal a plough or a ploughshare or a yoke or anything else, pay damages according to the number of days from the day when the theft took place, twelve folles for each day.

63. Let those who burn another's cart or steal it, pay twice its value.

64. Let those who set fire to a threshing-floor or stacks of corn by way of vengeance on their enemies be burnt.

65. Let those who set fire to a place where hay or chaff is kept, have a hand cut off.

66. If people pull down others' houses lawlessly and spoil their fences, on the ground that the others had fenced or built on their land, let them have their hands cut off.

67. If people take land on account of interest, and are proved to have been in enjoyment of it for more than seven years, let the judge take an account at the expiration of the seven years, and let him set down as principal the whole of the profits before and half the profits after.

68. If a man is found in a granary stealing corn, let him receive in the first place a hundred lashes, and make good the damage to the owner; if he is convicted a second time, let him pay twofold damages for his theft; if a third time, let him be blinded.

69. If a man at night steals wine from a jar or from a vat or out of

a butt, let him suffer the same penalty as is written in the chapter above.

70. If people have a deficient measure of corn and wine and do not follow the ancient tradition of their fathers but out of covetousness have unjust measures, contrary to those that are appointed, let them be beaten for their impiety.

71. If a man delivers cattle to a slave for pasture without his master's knowledge and the slave sells them or otherwise damages them, let the slave and his master go harmless.

72. If, with his master's knowledge, the slave receives beasts of any sort and eats them up or otherwise does away with them, let the slave's master indemnify the owner of the beasts.

73. If a man is passing on a road and finds a beast that is wounded or killed and out of pity gives information, but the owner of the beast suspects that the informer has played the rogue, let him take an oath concerning the wounding, but concerning the killing let no one be examined.

74. Where a man destroys another's beast on any pretence, when he is recognized, let him indemnify its owner.

75. Let him who destroys a sheepdog by poison receive a hundred lashes and give double the dog's value to its master; if the flock too is destroyed, let the slayer make good the whole loss, because he was the cause of the dog's destruction. And let testimony be given as to the dog, and if he fought with wild beasts, let it be as we have already said; but if he was an ordinary average dog, let his slayer be beaten and give the dog's value once only.

76. If two dogs are fighting and the master of one gives it to the other dog with a sword or a stick or a stone and by reason of that blow it is blinded or killed or suffers some other detriment, let him make it good to its master and receive twelve lashes.

77. If a man has a powerful dog which is arrogant towards its mates and he irritates his powerful dog against the weaker dogs and it happens that a dog is maimed or killed, let him make it good to its master and receive twelve lashes.

78. If a man harvests his lot before his neighbour's lots have been harvested and he brings in his beasts and does harm to his neighbours, let him receive thirty lashes and make good the damage to the party injured.

79. If a man gathers in the fruits of his vineyard and while the fruits

of some lots are still ungathered brings in his beasts, let him receive thirty lashes and make good the damage to the party injured.

80. If a man lawlessly, when he has a suit with another, cuts his vines or any other tree, let his hand be cut off.

81. If a man who is dwelling in a district ascertains that a piece of common ground is suitable for the erection of a mill and appropriates it and then, after the completion of the building, if the commonalty of the district complain of the owner of the building as having appropriated common ground, let them give him all the expenditure that is due to him for the completion of the building and let them share it in common with its builder.

82. If after the land of the district has been divided, a man finds in his own lot a place which is suitable for the erection of a mill and sets about it, the farmers of the other lots are not entitled to say anything about the mill.

83. If the water which comes to the mill leaves dry cultivated plots or vineyards, let him make the damage good; if not, let the mill be idle.

84. If the owners of the cultivated plots are not willing that the water go through their plots, let them be entitled to prevent it.

85. If a farmer finds one man's ox in another's vineyard doing damage and does not give notice to its owner, but, while he tries to chase it, kills or injures it, or fixes it on a stake, let him pay its whole value as damages.

C. The Struggle for the Peasant

18. *First Law of Romanus I (A.D. 922)*

J. and P. Zepos, eds., *Jus Graecoromanum,* I (Athens, 1931), 198–204. Translated by the editor.

New Law of Romanus [I] and Constantine [VII] and Christopher the Christ-loving and great autocrats and emperors, concerning alienation of property, and preference for relatives and joint owners and intermingled and adjacent joint taxpayers and jointly united and recognized co-payers of villages and hamlets, and punishment of powerful persons, and alienation of military properties. Published in the month of April, Indication X, [year] 6430 [A.D. 922].

There is an old law that no one should be hindered by relatives or joint owners in selling to whomever he wishes; another law forbids outright that one be allowed to sell to anyone save only inhabitants of his own mother-village. But we, giving much forethought to our own taxpayers and public taxes, as well as their other military and civil obligation and joint tax, in a clear and brief regulation [are] emending their apparent contradiction and imprecision by this our sacred mandate:

1. In every city and country and province from now on we command that if any persons who perchance have by inheritance either divisibly or indivisibly, or by common purchase or by any other such possession, or who have by inheritance or by new acquisition a dwelling in common or field or vineyard or other such immovable property [held in common] or otherwise not by common right [have lands] intermingled in some part in the neighboring properties or are joint taxpayers situated nearby or simply are nearby, should wish to alienate their own property by sale or lease or hire, let them not first alienate it to any other unless they notify those whom we name in order of preference. First let close relatives on either side [of the family] be summoned, then joint owners thus bound together; after them those [having] intermixed [lands], even if they are entirely strange to the person ceding [the land]; then neighboring fellow taxpayers; then those [having lands which are] simply joined by contact in some portion. By fellow taxpayers we mean all those enrolled upon the same taxed area, even if their own taxes are paid in different places. When many share boundaries with the property which is being given up, let preferential right be fulfilled by notification to each according to the same order, so that when those with preference have been invited, those called in succession should, if they wish, make a bargain. Then if all come by equal privileges, so that for this invitation none should be preferred to another, let the announcement be made identically to all who, having paid immediately within thirty days the just price or what a truthful buyer would prudently give from themselves or from some source, would receive it. Any who offer the price fixed for these but not

within the stated time will no longer have the right of preference, unless one of them is a prisoner or banished or expelled, or has honestly been absent on public or private business, or had not yet completed the twenty-fifth year of his age. Of these, those who received within four months possession of what belongs to them enter on a similar condition with new purchasers who live nearby, paying them in full the suitable price with lawful interest and necessary expenses; but let them completely expel purchasers from outside, giving them the price with their interest and costs. But if the financial managers of these said persons [outsiders] think that they should in no wise believe acceptable what has been done by these, by a written legal judgment let them [outsiders] be cast out or receive a contract [of lease-holding for the property]. But if they should be careless about this, let them render them the whole profit and gain from their own pocket, which they would have had if they had sought for the contract. And these things are for relatives and joint owners and fellow taxpayers and other nearby owners. But let this also be much more valid for the collective taxpayers of the said villages or hamlets, so that their owners should have preference to others. If all to whom preference is given beg off, or if there are shown causes of material damage or physical treachery or crude disgrace by the seller and his family, not by accident but by intention, which have come from themselves [the sellers] or those belonging to them, when someone has unwillingly endured such things, in no wise do we desire them to be brought into his property. All natives and outsiders are allowed to sell on the excuse of gift or prenuptial or simple present or gift on occasion of death or of testament or exchange or settlement: lest only on some excuse secretly selling or renting to those who do not have preference, let one allege to give or bequeath or any of the said things in public. Therefore those having the right of preference can demand an oath of the seller and buyer. But if those making the sale dare to do anything contrary to the text of our legislation and openly allege something else, should they be proved false after the oath, those dealing deceitfully with them shall undergo the penalties of forswearing, the one shall be deprived of his possession, the other of the price which he had secretly paid, and both these things shall be confiscated for the treasury, so that they may be transferred by the treasury to those next in succession. If they should be detected practicing something such before the oath, what they did shall be invalid, and the one who once attempted evilly to alienate the property shall be required to sell it against his will to those to whom we have accorded preference.

2. We prohibit for the future the powerful to take anything from the lowly by form of adoption as a son or simple gift or on the occasion of death either by testament or by usage alone or as if by some patronage and agreement, unless they are relatives. Nor are they to make new purchases or rents or exchanges from their owners in villages or hamlets in which they do not have their own properties. If the estates [*proasteia*] to be sold are not plots of their own, but of other persons, and if so-called klasmatic [abandoned] lands or other property belonging to it are to be sold by the treasury, even so let those owners have preference. When these voluntarily decline, then it is permitted to deal with the powerful. Let those be considered powerful who are capable of terrifying sellers, some not by themselves but by the authority of others, with whom they are conversationally intimate, or who on the excuse of beneficence offer them full security. If any of the powerful personages attempts to carry out any such thing, he shall be deprived of the property and stripped of the price by the treasury. But when after ten years nothing is alleged against those making deals in any way or receiving gifts or acquiring anything by testament by any of those given preference here, there shall be an investigation by the treasury.

3. In addition to these things we command that all military possessions [*stratiotika ktemata*] which have been alienated in any fashion within thirty years or are about to be alienated after this, should be returned without payment for the duty and service of their own military obligation [*strateia*], unless after the alienation enough remains to the soldier [*stratiotes*] as suffices for the one serving for the fulfillment of a fresh campaign. Insofar as it lacks [this], the alienation is annulled. [The genuineness of this paragraph has been challenged.]

19. *Second Law of Romanus I (A.D. 934)*

Zepos, *Jus*, I, 205–14. Translated by the editor.

New Law of Emperor Lord Romanus the Elder concerning invasions of the powerful into communal properties of the poor.

Iambic verses [found in all manuscripts]: Lord Romanus has made a new law which he has sent as redemption for those suffering injustice.

In the month of September, Indiction VIII, from the founding of the world year 6443 [934], Romanus [I], Constantine [VII], Stephen, and Constantine, faithful-in-God emperors of the Romans.

[The summary of the law's contents is omitted.]

[Prologue:] It is worthy of imitation and desirable for men, by whom the skill of the all-creating Hand is considered and named great and venerable, to adapt their spiritual condition toward imitation of the Guide; but for those by whom this has been accounted neither great nor blessed, the command of judgment exists to check them with training, and there remains for those who undertake the whole of life on earth and choose to live on earth alone that they be shown their own conduct [of life]. Thence is the great confusion of affairs, thence the great infliction of injustices, thence is the great and long misery of the poor [*ptochoi*] and the great moaning of the humble [*penetes*] for whom the Lord has arisen. For I shall arise for the sake of the misery of the poor and the groans of the downtrodden, says the Lord.[1] If God who created and preserves and rules us is arisen for vengeance, how will He overlook or forget us in the end? Does the poor man then await only the eyes of the empire for aid? Therefore for their justification looking not only to cure what was lately done and undertaken against them, but also applying a general and enduring healing to the matter, we have published the present law, preparing it as a banishment and cleansing of greedy intention, so that none of our people be driven abroad, the poor man be not oppressed, as something beneficial to the common good, acceptable to God, profitable to the treasury, and useful to the state, having considered it to be advantageous. Care for this subject did not previously escape notice nor is it inappropriate; through it regulations and decisions to check criminality of purpose and repress the grasp of the greedy hand came down constantly for all the provinces ordained beneath us. But since evil is multiform and extremely diversified, and all—but not least greed, if not rather more—contrive to escape the grasp of laws and regulations and think nothing of the unforgetting eye of divine justice, therefore these things now require more secure and careful codification, casting aside and removing the deceptions of the evildoers' plan.

[1] Psalms 11:6 (Septuagint) = 12:6 (King James).

1. Therefore we command that in every region and province which after God our power directs, the inhabitants have their appointed dwelling free and undisturbed. If his lifetime lasts in possession of it [the property], let it be the property of the children's and relatives' inheritance, or [let] the intention of the owner's will be fulfilled. But if, as [happens] in the course of human life and time's reversals, with necessity or need pressing or perhaps only desire suggesting [it], he partially or totally undertakes alienation of his own lands, let the right of purchase belong to the inhabitants of the same or neighboring fields or village lands. We do not lay down these laws out of hatred or jealousy of the more powerful, but we command it out of good will and protection of the poor [*penetes*] and for the common salvation. For instead of these things they used to declare that those happening to rule from God, surpassing the multitude in glory and wealth, did not pay much attention to the poor, because they abused those who did not already possess these things [glory and wealth], considering them as food. If such an unholy deed is not for everyone, then let the protection of law be common to all, lest the tare hidden in the wheat escape notice. Then none of the distinguished magistri or patricians [high court ranks], nor of those honored with governorships or generalships or civil or military ranks, nor of those reckoned in the senate [now an assembly of officials], nor of the thematic governors or subgovernors, nor of the very pious metropolitans or archbishops or bishops or abbots or ecclesiastical dignitaries or those having protection and supervision of pious and imperial foundations, either for their own person or for imperial or ecclesiastical profit, either through themselves or through a substituted person, shall ever dare completely or partially to steal into village land or field, by reason of purchase or gift or inheritance or any other excuse whatsoever. Therefore when such an invalid acquisition has been detected let them be ordered to retire without payment from their seizures with any added improvement in favor of the owners, or, when these and their relatives are not at hand, in favor of the inhabitants of the village lands or fields. For the authority of such persons has exulted over the great misery of the poor, by the number of their servants, their hirelings, and those otherwise attending and accompanying their prominent positions, [authority] which brings in prosecutions, forced services, other following oppressions and distresses, and has introduced no little destruction of the common good for those able to perceive, unless the present law

first checks it. For the habitation of the multitude shows the great profit of its employment, the collective contribution of the taxes, the joint rendering of military services, which will be entirely lacking when the common people have perished. It is necessary to get rid of those who keep [us] from civil stability and of the troublemaker, and to eject the harmful person and to contrive benefit of the common good. And hereafter let due measure maintain these things for the common profit and condition of our subjects. But it is needful to apply the approved cure not only for those who are to come but also for those who have come already. For many, taking as the starting point of trade [*alternate reading:* of wealth] the poverty of the poor [*penetes*], which time bringing all things has brought, or rather the multitude of our sins driving out divine mercy has introduced in place of benevolence, pity, kindness, [they] seeing the poor oppressed with hunger have cheaply bought up the properties of the unlucky poor, some with silver, some with gold, some with grain or other offerings, being more violent than the impending suffering, and in those times thereafter being like a pestilential influx of diseases for the wretched inhabitants of the villages, or in the manner of a gangrene fastening on the body of the villages and inflicting utter destruction.

2. Then from the past first indiction [i.e., September 927–August 928], to wit from the famine occurring or passing, whoever of the distinguished persons, whom the present law designated above to be excluded, has become possessed of fields or village lands or has partially or completely gained properties in them, let them be thrust out therefrom, recovering the price paid by them either from the original owners or their heirs or relatives, or when these are without means from other joint taxpayers or else from the collective unit organized for paying the price. Regarding improvements by them, when these said persons are able and willing to pay the fitting [price], or when they are incapable and unwilling, return the materials to those who are being restored, although they added them by their own expenditures, and these are not to be displayed as evidence of the wealth and profit of the poor. But so much concerning seemingly probable just possession by purchase. But we declare that both former and present gifts or inheritances or other such-like tricky acquisitions or seizures are invalid, that they are to make no further inquiries regarding these powerful evildoers, but freely to restore these things to their proper owners, or when perchance these have vanished from mankind, to their

children or relatives, or when these too are gone, to render them to their fellow taxpayers.

3. If decrees of divine providence regard some persons more favorably or change for others by incomprehensible reasons the condition of the present life to a better one, which [providence] leads them away from a lower fortune and raises them to higher, we adjudge that they remain in the inheritance and condition which they enjoyed at the beginning, and not, while extending the measure of their own fortune, complete plundering their less fortunate neighbors. For this accusation against those who take pride in the elevation and glory of their earthly splendor is more appropriate for the more humble of their contracts: distinction of persons [by wealth and rank] not for common or profitable or mutual dealing, not only in scheming minds but also in the pursuit of affairs, is daily formed and affirmed in many cases. To those who rather say they observe the decrees of divine favor toward themselves, let them treat more favorably with their fellow villager, and considering the inscrutability of fortune and the inevitability of [divine] judgment, let them not seize their neighbor's goods, unless they wish to be punished with the foregoing sentence.

4. As for those who before the specified time [i.e., before 927] came into possession of such properties, although they are observed remaining in the same condition, we allow them to remain so, subject equally with the others to the prohibition of neighboring acquisition. If some are shown to be burdensome and oppressive to their neighbors, contriving heavy and unceasing injuries for the poor, let them be thrust forth and expelled, receiving banishment from their own possessions as the reward of a harsh and insatiable policy.

5. The repayment of prices specified above [clause 2], needs well-proportioned and delicate investigation, not careless and thoughtless judgment. For when a free and unforced sale has been made and rightful payment of the price observed, the reckoning for recovery, which overcomes the harshness of poverty for someone, shall justly be maintained by a small addition of the law. Let recovery and restitution of the lands immediately be made to those who sold it or their heirs or relatives, but when these no longer live, to the fellow taxpayers; if these were valid deals, let the price paid at the beginning be restored, but if invalid, let them not be pressed for speed of repayment, lest the presently inflicted payment should seem more burdensome and grievous to them than the profit and security which are expected for the fu-

ture. Otherwise on account of speedy restitution the cunning and stinginess of the people's mind will not blush to help in planning the escape of those who have formed an intention thereto. By those given to such gain by the passion of greed and by spiritual poverty, and deeming shameful none of those [practices] contributing to business and overladen with a generous supply of such meddling, nothing shall be left unattempted, nothing untried for the planned end of their own purpose. But for the hindrance of new tricks and the fulfillment of what has been ordained, let a period of three years of delay [for repayment] be established, [a period] capable of bringing wealth to the poor man and preserved for offering the repurchase price without penalty. For along with advantage one ought to interweave and add benevolence to legislation, and especially by an added delay of time. For when once prohibition concerning these things has been published, those caught in disobedience of established laws are to profit by nothing strange or foreign in the punishment of their crimes, nor be deprived of the present judgments. For always mingling harshness of precision in a benevolent judgment, instead of present expulsion we have commanded the delay of three years, checking sinners in due measure, but deservedly benefiting by delay and comforting the poor [*penetes*] who are worthy to enjoy mercy, and applying and performing the cure appropriate for each.

6. Then we have heard that some have advanced to so much desire of profits, so that they deliberately choose to buy cheaply (but how could I say that, and not [say] greedily gulp?) the properties of the poor. The distinction of intention and action has not produced a like distinction among graspers. If the just value of what has been sold is found [to be] over double [the price], let the purchasers be expelled without payment.

7. But if it [the just value] is not up to so much [double the price], yet is likewise for defrauding and injury of the sellers, and the profit from the income thereof has already equaled the amount of the price, let them demand nothing else. But when it [the profit] was less, let them recover the rest [of the price] from those receiving their rights for deprivation of lands.

8. Then when one becomes a monk for appearance's sake or wishes to become a monk and confirms his own property to the holy monastery, let not things which then seemed excellent receive any violation. Enjoying appropriate benefit from the present decree, let [the monas-

tery] receive the just price of the property, if this [act] was truly done for the sake of salvation and not for a trick and deception and false purpose. This will be counted no less for the benefit of the holy establishments than of the poor, since [the former] are released from strife and rivalries and slavish property, while [the latter] are avoiding and not encountering the causes of disasters, [to wit] discoveries [of old titles by monasteries?] and constraints, so let it [property] remain for [support of] men living and still bound in the flesh, and not for those uncorrupted persons who have been entrusted with human sins.

These things then have been ordained very beneficently, both reproving very moderately the insatiable greed of covetousness and furthering the common profit, so that none of the distinguished magistri or patricians, nor of those honored with commands or authorities or any sort of imperial rank, nor of the civil or military or thematic governors or subgovernors, nor of the metropolitans or archbishops or bishops or abbots or heads of pious establishments, nor of any others enjoying worldly or priestly rank, should ever by purchase or gift or in any other fashion creep secretly into possessions of village lands or fields. We command that those who after the present regulation desired to undertake any such thing be expelled therefrom without compensation and be deprived of their own additions and improvements and, when they are distinguished persons, pay the price of the acquisition to the public treasury (not for the sake of the profit or revenue of the treasury—for how could we, who are eager to check the insatiable desire of others' greed, unblushingly command something for our own profit, thus being reproached for accomplishing not the common good but our own?—but for the consolation of the poor), while meaner persons are also expelled without compensation and taught wisdom by the appropriate punishment. We wish these things to prevail for the salvation of our subjects, regarding whom great and ceaseless care is imposed on us. For if we have devoted so much care for those under our power as to spare none of the things which contribute toward freedom, whereby, with God assisting, lands and villages and cities have come to us from the enemy, some coming by act of war, others rushing in by their example and from fear of capture which seized them before the martial trumpet [Romanus I had won important victories in Asia Minor]; with God assisting we have striven to extend this freedom from hostile incursion to our subjects, while we preferred the work of prayer and study. Then when we had done so much concerning the attack of external enemies, how should we not rid ourselves of those domestic internal enemies of nature, of creation, of good order, by the righteous purpose of liberty, by the cutting sword of the present legislation and liberty, scorning and oppressing insatiate desire, cutting off the greedy purpose, and freeing the subject from the yoke of the tyrannical and oppressive hand and scheme? Let each of those who happens to be a judge constantly maintain these things by his own strength, for the service of God and of our empire [which is] from Him, for common profit and benefit.

20. *Law of Nicephorus II Phocas Regarding Property (A.D. 966–967)*

Zepos, *Jus,* I, 253–55. Translated by the editor.

New law of the Emperor Nicephorus, which Symeon the patrician and chief secretary dictated, regarding how the powerful [*dynatoi*] were to be preferred to the poor [*penetes*] in the purchase of things sold by the powerful.

The just Father who created equally all His children, the Yoke of Justice, and the straight Rule and precise Regulation, our Lord and God, Who is neither biased nor judges inequitably, but rather by concern for all alike, has prepared heaven and earth and those things contained therein for all. Therefore it behooves those enjoying imperial power to imitate Him the more, and to maintain equity for all those under their power and to provide for all in common, because they have been called lawful authorities by former legislators[1] and a common and equitable good. Since those who ruled before us have published legislation regarding the need which existed at that time, preventing the powerful from buying the possessions of the poor and of soldiers [*stratiotes*] and doing well [thereby], but in it they added that the poor received preference for the property of the powerful, not

[1] Basil I, *Epanagoge,* II, 1, in Ernest Barker, *Social and Political Thought in Byzantium from Justinian I to the Last Palaeologus* (London: Oxford University Press, 1957), p. 89.

only by right of co-ownership, but also from joint taxpaying, and they entirely shut out those who are daily increasing, not giving them any sort of opening for acquisition, but rather causing those who are already well-provided to live in confinement and difficulty on account of the fact that the poor had preference in purchasing, and not thinking at all about their security but rather, so to speak, thereby not allowing them to remain on their own [properties], they seemed biased and by this command they brought to nothing and destroyed the whole of Roman power. What is eagerly desired has not been gained on account of the weakness which exists everywhere. Our authority, which is zealous to maintain and preserve equitable legislation for all, not overturning that legislation by the law enunciated below, but rather creating equity and stability in it, has at the tenth indiction [September 966–August 967] clearly pronounced as follows.

1. We decree the legislation published by previous emperors to be in force and we confirm it in everything, except in this alone do we command it to be void, that the poor are not to be preferred in regard to the property of a lender [*daneistes,* possibly a misreading for *dynastes,* powerful man] which is for sale, neither as a result of joint tax responsibility nor co-proprietorship, if *stratiotai* [military landholders] or civil [personages] are to be found. We command that the personage in authority again receive possession of it, to wit the one [personage] who appeared for the tranquility and succor of the poor [*penetes*] situated adjacent to it, and let him who was minded, after becoming possessed of the property, to injure the neighbors be expelled as a violent and evil man not only from the acquisition but also from his hereditary lands. We wish that the powerful [*dynatoi*] make purchases only from powerful, the *stratiotai* and poor [*penetes*] from those having a similar status. And just as we prohibit these from purchasing the goods of the powerful, so we forbid again those from making purchases from the poor [*penetes*] and from needy *stratiotai,* nor are they to cite joint tax responsibility or co-ownership against justice, for which [justice] we make law for all, not caring about some more and others less.

2. Since the course of forty years [the period since the famine of 927–928 within which, according to Constantine VII's law, the *stratiotai* might recover lands then illegally obtained from them] passing without accusation or complaint has confirmed the right of those holding possessions alienated by *stratiotai,* but [legal] hindering and chal-

lenging by complaints burdened those who made acquisitions before the famine [before 927], and being sued indiscriminately has often caused them to be deprived of these things: we command that those who are found to have made acquisition in good faith from *stratiotai* or civil [persons] before the year of the famine remain undisturbed, and the forty year period and challenging by complaints thereon are not to be valid, nor is their ownership to be undermined or transferred at all, unless they made acquisitions by seizure and by forceful occupation and bad faith, as if rushing upon enemies and desiring more in addition. What was then commanded by the old law [of Leo VI] regarding sale will after this be annulled and overturned by the legislation published regarding the famine.

21. *Law of Nicephorus II Phocas Regarding Military Lands (A.D. 963–969)*

Zepos, *Jus,* I, 255–56. Translated by the editor.

Regarding *stratiotai* who have alienated their properties, then desired them back.

The *protospatharius* [first sword-bearer, a rank in court] Basil, in charge of petitions [a post in the administration], has represented [to us] that he freely restores to *stratiotai* lands which have been recovered [from purchasers], because they have been found performing military service for these same places; and he has shown that this seems to be hard, not to have authority to sell anything from the lands belonging to someone anywhere, whatever and however much property he owns.

1. Therefore up to the present moment we desire that for *stratiotai* who sold their fields such a law be in force, that for the *stratiotes* a profitable immovable property of four pounds [worth of gold] was ordained on account of his military service [i.e., to support himself, his horse, and his equipment]; if one having this [stratiotic property] has been found selling another property elsewhere and now seeks it back, [we wish] that he be able to recover it by [his legal] preferential right, except not without payment, but on deposit of the just price. But if he

sold any part of the four pounds' [worth] of profitable immovable property, let him recover this without repayment.

2. But from now on, when the property of mail-clad and armored men receives transfer, we command that no simple *stratiotes* can alienate elsewhere immovable property from this in security, if he does not have in addition profitable immovable property [worth] twelve pounds [of gold]. But if he has sold anything out of such property which totals up to thus much, let him recover without repayment. If, having anything beyond this (to wit, the twelve pounds' worth), he has sold it, then requests it back, let him not recover it freely, but render the appropriate price.

22. *Law of Basil II Regarding Peasant Properties (A.D. 996)*

Zepos, *Jus,* I, 262–72. Translated by the editor.

New legislation of the pious Emperor Basil the Younger, regarding the powerful [*dynatoi*] acquiring property from the poor [*penetes*], forbidding them from the first legislation of Emperor Romanus the Elder [Lecapenus], to wit from the second indiction, year 6437 [September 928–August 929].

1. Whereas our empire [Byzantine form for Our Majesty], by the grace of God from Whom it [i.e., we] takes its [our] imperial origin, has undertaken to investigate the lawsuits brought by the rich and the poor, it has found that the powerful [*dynatoi*] who greedily desire to expand have a fair excuse for their private lust, the period of up to forty years, and that they eagerly desire to pass through this [period] either by offerings and gifts or by the force available to them and then to have in full ownership what they have wickedly grasped from the poor [*penetes*], it has published the present law, which thus corrects what preceded and checks the present-day powerful and hinders those coming hereafter from attacking them [the poor], knowing that they [the poor] would find no help thereof, but not only will they be deprived of the other person's property, but also their children and whomever they leave it to. From what we wish to say it will be evident

that our empire does not imprudently or without examination overthrow ownership [established] by [long] time, but [we] have pity on the poor and consider the common good and its condition and embrace righteousness and cure the terrible passion of greed. For we have been much disturbed on this account by the poor [*ptochoi*], and passing through the *themes* [provinces] of our empire and going on expeditions we have seen with our own eyes the acts of greed and injustice daily inflicted on them. For how, as has happened, shall time be absolutely efficacious, when one who is powerful practices greed against the poor man, being mighty and prosperous he will gain a long period of time, and will transmit his power and prosperity to his successors? Perchance he is a patrician, or else a descendant of one, will he not prevail in power and transmit power to his descendants? And perhaps he is a magister [high court rank] and domestic of the schools [commander of the palace guard], or else their descendants who are likewise powerful and who have intimate acquaintance with emperors and have their prosperity extending back as far as seventy or a hundred years. Then shall we not hinder them, and affirm the right belonging to the poor, of which they were basely robbed and defrauded? For when one who happens to be a powerful man acquired property in communities of village lands or paid for more, and when his successors received his authority along with his wealth and gave no room for the poor man for taking [legal] action against them regarding what they had vilely carried off and pillaged from him, it is manifestly clear that however much time has passed in these cases, the poor man shall not be prevented from requesting and recovering his own property. Should we not do this, we would give an excuse to the grasping individual to say that, since today I am well off and the poor man is not able to act against me, if my son prospers and through our success the time ordained in the laws passes, or I last out the time in prosperity, we hold the property irrecoverably, and greed is profitable to me. [*Marginal note, perhaps by the emperor:* This is clear from the family of the Maleïni, and likewise of the Phocases. For the patrician Constantine Maleïnus and his son the magister Eustathius enjoyed wealth which extended back from them a hundred or even a hundred twenty years. The Phocases much more than they, for their grandfather, then the father, and thereafter his sons had, so to speak, almost perpetual authority up to our day. And how shall such as these have time coming to their aid?] But again shall we not reckon as powerful also the originally powerless poor man who is later honored and raised to a height of glory and prosperity? He was powerless while he belonged to those lower down [in the social scale], and we allowed time to aid him; but he was powerful from the moment he was deemed worthy of rank, and we shall prove that time should not benefit him. Such things are often seen happening in our day, and one has recently been discovered by us. For we have discovered Philocales, who at the beginning was one of the poor villagers, but later distinguished and wealthy. While he belonged to the lower orders, he paid taxes along with his fellow villagers and did them no harm; but from when God raised him to the rank of *hebdomadarius* [or *hebdomarius,* page in the imperial bedchamber], then *koitonites* [chamberlain], and thereafter *protovestiarius* [chief chamberlain], he obtained his whole village and made it his private domain [*proasteion*], even altering the said village's name. Then since he has thus been elevated and so carries on his affairs, is it possible that we should grant him [the legal] period [of delay] for his assistance and allow him to have what he has wickedly plundered? Not a bit. Wherefore our empire passing by the place and learning of the matter from the complaint of the poor, has overthrown his costly structures down to the foundation, and restored their own possessions to the poor, but has left him the property which he had in the beginning, and made him again one of the villagers. Not only should such persons be reckoned as powerful, but also all those embraced and successively inscribed in the regulation of our grandsire Emperor Romanus the Elder [the patricians, magistri, etc., of the law of 934]. [*Marginal note, perhaps by the emperor:* He named the palace guardsmen themselves powerful, while we call these powerful, we also add the chief centurions: for we have already in practice recognized them as powerful.] Therefore we ordain by our present law that property acquired by the powerful in communities of village land up to the first law of our grandsire Emperor Romanus the Elder, which [property] has certainty from written privileges and confirming witnesses, is to be maintained and be in their hands, just as pronounced by former laws. For on this account we desire written privileges and confirmatory witnesses to be brought forward, lest the powerful by subtlety make the excuse that properties recently acquired by them belong to them by written contract from a long time back. But from then up to now, which is the first of January of the ninth indiction, year 6504 [996], and in the future, since the written command was issued by the published law of our grandfather Emperor Romanus the Elder, neither the whole [forty-year elapsed] time is valid nor does any part of the whole have effect against the poor when they have to do with the powerful, but let their possessions be restored to the poor, nor [let anything be said] regarding recovery of the prices or the justified improvements of the powerful, because they have been found transgressing the said law and are instead worthy to be corrected. For the said emperor, our grandfather Romanus the Elder, writing and saying that: "From now on I forbid the powerful to make acquisitions in the communities of villages," showed that he forbade them throughout the age and to infinity, and he did not accord them a period of time for assistance [i.e., a period after which an illicit expropriation would be legalized]. Not only do we ordain this for the future, as specified, but we also make this law retroactive to the past year which we specified. For if we shall not correct whatever past events are now called in question, how would future ones be guarded against, and persons hereafter be made afraid? [*Marginal note, perhaps by the emperor:* How can they cease from doing such things? For this is more difficult than anything else, because the powerful leave properties assembled by seizure and greed to their children, thinking that in expectation of the forty-year period they have undisputed ownership of such things. When such aid, to wit from the forty-year period, is removed, the children of the powerful who are deprived of such an inheritance won by greed, which [inheritance] they received from their fathers, come down to poverty and utter destitution, such as the grandsons of the magister Romanus Mousele suffered from our empire. For while these had at Philomelion so much wealth left them by their grandfather and fathers, they too came down to poverty. Then our empire, which cuts down such injustice and inequality, and which determines the rights belonging to all rich and poor, has removed the period of forty years, so that the powerful who are aware of this do not leave such an inheritance to their children, but the poor deprived of their property should not despair, but should have firm assistance from the present law for the recovery of their property.]

2. Since we have found many subjects in surveys registered in *chrysobulls* [imperial grants], and many such matters have been acted upon before our tribunal, we command that surveys brought forward in evidence have no force, nor shall those proffering them have any legal right from the uncertainty occurring from them. For they are not is-

sued by imperial knowledge or purpose, but by that of the recipients; again, not even the chief secretaries who recorded the *chrysobulls* are on the spot and observe when the measurement or their publication takes place. Therefore as stated we wish those in which doubt occurs to be invalid and have no effect. But if such surveys happen to be in the records of the treasury department or in other confirmatory privileges, we order them to be heeded and observed. [*Marginal note, perhaps by the emperor:* It is written thus: Since many fields of the poor are found included in the surveys of *chrysobulls,* notwithstanding imperial documents, and because those receiving *chrysobulls* thereof hold such fields on the excuse of the survey, things which our empire, while occupied with military expeditions, has found in almost the whole of the East and the whole West: it is commanded that such surveys have no validity whatsoever, and that those proffering them have no legal right from the uncertainty occurring from them. Nor do such surveys come from our empire, as when it had their complete possession it ruled them firm and unchangeable, but our empire made the gift by *chrysobull,* while the surveys were made by others, they cannot have trustworthiness, certitude, and security equal to the force of a *chrysobull.*] . . .

4. In addition to these things we decree that against the treasury there is no time limit which cuts short its own right, but let one invoke something from Caesar Augustus and receive justice regarding its recovery [i.e., against a claim of ownership by the treasury, title had to be proved back to Augustus]. For there are many things inducing it [the treasury] to seek out its property everywhere: first, one cannot be satisfied that the emperor who confirmed it considered and observed the whole matter on account of [his] great preoccupation and anxiety for public good and of being surrounded by numerous cares on every hand, and then [on account of] entrusting it to those who go out to the *themes* [provinces]. Wherefore it is manifest that however much such [provincial officials] did well and with justice and not for defrauding of the treasury shall be secure and confirmed; but however much [they did] falsely and for its deception shall remain invalid. But rather, if it is necessary to say anything in behalf of the treasury, when he who happens to rule desires, he should be able to investigate such matters with immunity and manage them as pleases him. But otherwise something will not have been discovered, because the forty-year period has passed uninterruptedly and no inspector or imperial [mes-

senger] has come out seeking the treasury's right. But if such a person, who is sent for proof and recovering of the rights of the treasury, being found greedy and deceitful, neglects recovering and rescuing them, but he rather appears a betrayer of its rights for [his] greedy and villainous purpose, [then] the treasury, which never ceased to seek out its own right, will not lose its case thereby. And in fact our empire has found this by very deeds, because the inspectors and those otherwise provided by the treasury and dispatched for duties work numerous frauds against it, and few are found who fulfill our commands. . . .

7. Finally we wish that what has been disputed about the right of fairs have proper order. For since some have been left in want, charging that, while they formerly had a fair established on their own lands, the dealers who organized the fair withdrew and departed from them, and left the former proprietors of the fair deserted, but created a new fair in the lands of those who received them. We command that if such a thing ever occurs, if all the fairmen and merchants both native and immigrant [from outside the district] remove at once and with one accord from the former owner of the fair, but come to other lands creating anew the fair, they can do so unhindered and free, should they desire to make a transfer of place of the fair, not being compelled but being voluntarily and by their own choice brought to it. But if there is dissension among the fairmen and some choose to be in the places where they formerly held the fair, but the rest withdraw and transfer to other places, then let the disagreement be settled by priority of time, and, however many they are, let those who withdrew rather be joined to the union of those choosing [to remain], and let the ancient privilege of the place prevail. And since removals or transfers of fairs have a fourfold division (for transfers are customarily either from powerful to powerful, or from weak to weak, or from powerful to weak, or from weak to powerful), what has already been commanded shall have effect only for the three first cases, to wit for transfers from powerful to powerful, and from weak to weak, and from powerful to weak. The fourth heading will obtain our more personal and beneficent interpretation. For since there is a great inclination in the powerful toward withdrawal of fairs from the rightful [owners, the] weak, we decree that in this case this withdrawal is not to occur, to wit the transfer of the fair from weak to powerful, unless the whole [fair] with one accord voluntarily withdraws and transfers from one

place to another where it was formerly long established, since two good reasons combine here, the right of priority and the conflux and agreement of the whole crowd. For, if in the other three cases one good reason being alone seemed to be sufficient, to wit only agreement, when the whole fair transferred, or only temporal priority, to wit when the fair divided and split in two, but in this fourth case we command that there be a combination of the two reasons in order to validate the transfer of fairs from weak to powerful, the stated agreement of everyone and the right of priority. [Thus are we] extending every means as aid to the poor and removing the excess of might of the powerful, something which also was formerly excellently cared for by our [great] grandfather the blessed Emperor Lord Romanus the Elder regarding alienations of rightful immovable property of the weak to the powerful.

Part Four

❦ CONSTANTINOPLE

While dependent on the products of the countryside, the Byzantine Empire was never wholly rural, but was dotted with small towns. Unlike most medieval Western kingdoms, it possessed a capital, Constantinople, which was the center of government and the focus of Byzantine life. In the "Great City," as the Byzantines called it, were Haghia Sophia, seat of the patriarch and center of the Byzantine church; the Great Palace (or Constantine's Palace), not merely the emperor's residence but also the location of government bureaus, treasuries, and arsenals; the hippodrome, focus of popular life; numerous churches and monasteries, which sheltered some of the most venerated relics in the Christian world; schools and "universities," which, after the loss of Alexandria and Antioch to the Arabs, preserved Greek literature; wharves and warehouses on the Golden Horn which made the city a great commercial center; shops which manufactured luxury products of worldwide fame; splendid forums, great town houses of the rich, and acres of slums. Although the population rarely exceeded two hundred thousand, Constantinople seemed enormous and wonderful to medieval travelers. Odo of Deuil, a monk who in 1147 accompanied Louis VII of France on the Second Crusade, wrote of the combination of splendor and poverty he had seen (Reading No. 23). Two decades later the Jewish traveler Benjamin of Tudela visited the city, and was struck by its thriving commerce, as well as by the mistreatment of the Jewish population of Pera, the suburb north of the Golden Horn (Reading No. 24).

The merchants and manufacturers of Constantinople worked under the supervision of the Eparch or Prefect of the city. Each trade and profession was organized into a guild responsible to him. The regulations governing the activities of some of these survive in the so-called "Book of the Prefect," a collection probably compiled in the tenth century from older materials. The rules regulated prices and profits, but assured a monopoly to the guild members. The bankers' code suggests the importance which the government attached to a sound currency, the rules for the victualers or grocers, its concern for the consumer (Reading No. 25). Partly because of this intense supervision, the Byzantines failed to develop an aggressive middle class which could compete with that of Western Europe in the twelfth and thirteenth centuries.

In his political calculations no emperor could afford to overlook the populace of the capital. Poor, frequently discontented, and given to turbulence, the people utilized the circus factions, Blues and Greens, to express their grievances. These parties originally supported rival chariots at the hippodrome, and later developed religious and social affiliations: in the sixth century, the Blues seem to have been orthodox and well-to-do, while the Greens were mainly poor people who leaned toward Monophysitism. At the hippodrome an aggrieved faction could appeal for redress to the emperor in his box, but dissatisfaction often burst forth in street rioting. In 532, Blues and Greens, moved apparently by recent high taxes, combined to oppose Justinian, and almost overthrew him; this "Nika" Riot was vividly recorded by Procopius, who, as a member of Belisarius' staff, seemingly witnessed it (Reading No. 26).

Six centuries later, while the factions had died out, the people could still be roused; their grievances were now more economic than political. By 1182, numerous Italian merchants had settled along the Golden Horn; these "Latins," in return for naval assistance to the empire, had received privileges and tax exemptions which enabled them to compete favorably with Byzantine merchants. As the native middle class lost ground, unemployment and chronic poverty spread among the masses, and they were ready to turn against the arrogant Latins. At this time, during the reign of the child Alexius II Comnenus, Andronicus Comnenus vied with his cousin Alexius Comnenus the Protosebastus for control of the government. Having brought an army from Asia Minor, Andronicus agreed with the leaders of the mob that they would seize and surrender Alexius the Protosebastus to him, and he would permit the people to vent their wrath upon the Latins. There followed the Latin Massacre of April 1182, in which thousands of innocent persons (including a cardinal) were mercilessly slaughtered. Many fled by sea, some to Syria, where Archbishop William of Tyre recorded their story (Reading No. 27). The hostility of the mob to the Latins reappeared in subsequent years, and contributed to the decision of the Westerners to seize the city.

A. The World Capital

23. *Odo of Deuil,* Journey of Louis VII to the East (*1147*)

Reprinted by permission of the publisher from Odo of Deuil, *De Profectione Ludovici VII in Orientem: The Journey of Louis VII to the East,* trans. Virginia G. Berry, Records of Civilization, Sources and Studies (New York: Columbia University Press, 1948), pp. 63–67.

Constantinople, the glory of the Greeks, rich in renown and richer still in possessions, is laid out in a triangle shaped like a ship's sail. In its inner angle stand Santa Sophia and Constantine's Palace, in which there is a chapel that is revered for its exceedingly holy relics. Moreover, Constantinople is girt on two sides by the sea; when approaching the city we had the Arm of St. George on the right and on the left a certain estuary, which, after branching from the Arm, flows on for about four miles. In that place the Palace of Blachernae, although having foundations laid on low ground, achieves eminence through excellent construction and elegance and, because of its surroundings on three sides, affords its inhabitants the triple pleasure of looking out upon sea, fields, and city. Its exterior is of almost matchless beauty, but its interior surpasses anything that I can say about it. Throughout it is decorated elaborately with gold and a great variety of colors, and the floor is marble, paved with cunning workmanship; and I do not know whether the exquisite art or the exceedingly valuable stuffs endows it with the more beauty or value. The third side of the city's triangle includes fields, but it is fortified by towers and a double wall which extends for about two miles from the sea to the palace. This wall is not very strong, and it possesses no lofty towers; but the city puts its trust, I think, in the size of its population and the long period of peace which it has enjoyed. Below the walls lies open land, cultivated by plough and hoe, which contains gardens that furnish the citizens all kinds of vegetables. From the outside underground conduits flow in, bringing the city an abundance of sweet water.

The city itself is squalid and fetid and in many places harmed by permanent darkness, for the wealthy overshadow the streets with buildings and leave these dirty, dark places to the poor and to travelers; there murders and robberies and other crimes which love the darkness are committed. Moreover, since people live lawlessly in this city, which has as many lords as rich men and almost as many thieves as poor men, a criminal knows neither fear nor shame, because crime is not punished by law and never entirely comes to light. In every respect she exceeds moderation; for, just as she surpasses other cities in wealth, so, too, does she surpass them in vice. Also, she possesses many churches unequal to Santa Sophia in size but equal to it in beauty, which are to be marveled at for their beauty and their many saintly relics. . . .

24. *Benjamin of Tudela,* Itinerary (*1160s*)

Reprinted by permission of the publisher, Oxford University Press, from Benjamin of Tudela, *Itinerary,* trans. Marcus Nathan Adler (London: Henry Frowde, Oxford University Press, 1907), pp. 12–14.

All sorts of merchants come here from the land of Babylon, from the land of Shinar, from Persia, Media, and all the sovereignty of the land of Egypt, from the land of Canaan, and the empire of Russia, from Hungaria, Patzinakia, Khazaria, and the land of Lombardy and Sepharad. It is a busy city, and merchants come to it from every country by sea or land, and there is none like it in the world except Bagdad, the great city of Islam. In Constantinople is the church of Santa Sophia, and the seat of the Pope of the Greeks, since the Greeks do not obey the Pope of Rome. There are also churches according to the number of the days of the year. A quantity of wealth beyond telling is brought hither year by year as tribute from the two islands and the castles and villages which are there. And the like of this wealth is not to be found in any other church in the world. And in this church there are pillars of gold and silver, and lamps of silver and gold more than a man can count. Close to the walls of the palace is also a place of amusement belonging to the king, which is called the Hippodrome, and every year on the anniversary of the birth of Jesus the king gives a great entertainment there. And in that place men from all the races of the world come before the king and queen with jugglery and without jugglery, and they introduce lions, leopards, bears, and wild asses, and they engage them in combat with one another; and the same thing is done with birds. No entertainment like this is to be found in any other land.

This King Emanuel built a great palace for the seat of his government upon the sea-coast, in addition to the palaces which his fathers built, and he called its name Blachernae. He overlaid its columns and walls with gold and silver, and engraved thereon representations of the battles before his day and of his own combats. He also set up a throne of gold and of precious stones, and a golden crown was suspended by a gold chain over the throne, so arranged that he might sit thereunder. It was inlaid with jewels of priceless value, and at night time no lights were required, for every one could see by the light which the stones gave forth. Countless other buildings are to be met with in the city. From every part of the empire of Greece tribute is brought here every year, and they fill strongholds with garments of silk, purple, and gold. Like unto these storehouses and this wealth, there is nothing in the whole world to be found. It is said that the tribute of the city amounts every year to 20,000 gold pieces, derived both from the rents of shops and markets, and from the tribute of merchants who enter by sea or land.

The Greek inhabitants are very rich in gold and precious stones, and they go clothed in garments of silk with gold embroidery, and they ride horses, and look like princes. Indeed, the land is very rich in all cloth stuffs, and in bread, meat, and wine.

Wealth like that of Constantinople is not to be found in the whole world. Here also are men learned in all the books of the Greeks, and they eat and drink every man under his vine and his fig-tree.

They hire from amongst all nations warriors called Loazim (Barbarians) to fight with the Sultan Masud, King of the Togarmim (Seljuks), who are called Turks; for the natives are not warlike, but are as women who have no strength to fight.

No Jews live in the city, for they have been placed behind an inlet of the sea. An arm of the sea of Marmora shuts them in on the one side, and they are unable to go out except by way of the sea, when they want to do business with the inhabitants. In the Jewish quarter are about 2,000 Rabbanite Jews and about 500 Karaïtes, and a fence divides them. Amongst the scholars are several wise men, at their head being the chief rabbi R. Abtalion, R. Obadiah, R. Aaron Bechor Shoro, R. Joseph Shir-Guru, and R. Eliakim, the warden. And amongst them there are artificers in silk and many rich merchants. No Jew there is allowed to ride on horseback. The one exception is R. Solomon Hamitsri, who is the king's physician, and through whom the Jews enjoy considerable alleviation of their oppression. For their condition is very low, and there is much hatred against them, which is fostered by the tanners, who throw out their dirty water in the streets before the doors of the Jewish houses and define the Jews' quarter (the Ghetto). So the Greeks hate the Jews, good and bad alike, and subject them to great oppression, and beat them in the streets, and in every way treat them with rigour. Yet the Jews are rich and good, kindly and charitable, and bear their lot with cheerfulness. The district inhabited by the Jews is called Pera.

B. The Directed Economy

25. *Book of the Prefect (tenth century)*

Reprinted by permission of the publisher from A. E. R. Boak, trans., "The Book of the Prefect," *Journal of Economic and Business History,* I (Cambridge, Mass.: Harvard University Press, 1928–1929), 605, 613–14.

THE BANKERS.

1. Anyone who wishes to be nominated as a banker must be vouched for by respected and honest men who will guarantee that he

will do nothing contrary to the ordinances; to wit, that he will not pare down, or cut, or put false inscriptions on *nomismata* or *miliarisia,* or set one of his own slaves in his place at his bank if he should happen to be occupied with some temporary duties, so that no trickery may thereby enter into the business of the profession. If anyone is caught in such practices, he shall be punished by the amputation of his hand.

2. The money-changers shall report to the Prefect the forgers who station themselves in the squares and streets in order to prevent them from indulging in illegal practices. If they know of such and fail to report them, they shall suffer the aforementioned punishment.

3. The money-changers shall make no deduction from the value of an unadulterated *miliarision* which bears the genuine royal stamp, but shall accept it as equivalent to twenty-four *obols.* However, if the condition of the coin is otherwise, it must be valued accordingly. Those who disregard this injunction shall be scourged, shorn, and suffer confiscation.

4. Each banker shall keep two assistants to sort his coins. He must go surety for these, so that if one of them is detected acting contrary to the ordinances both he and the one who appointed him shall suffer the aforesaid penalties.

5. Any money-changer who receives a counterfeited *nomisma* or *miliarision,* and fails to report it to the Prefect together with its possessor, shall be scourged, shorn, and banished.

6. The bankers must not give their subordinates account books or coins and station them in the squares and streets in order to receive the profit accruing from their activities. Even on occasions of distribution of largesses or the performance of services for the emperor they shall not go away and abandon their banks. If anyone is caught doing so, he shall be beaten, shorn, and suffer confiscation. . . .

The Victualers.

1. The victualers shall open their shops in the square and streets throughout the whole city so that the necessities of life may easily be found. They shall sell meat, pickled fish, meal, cheese, honey, olive oil, green vegetables of all sorts, butter, solid and liquid pitch, cedar resin, hemp, flax, plaster, pottery vessels, bottles, nails, and all the other things sold by a bar-balance and not by twin scales. They are for-

bidden to engage in the trades of the perfumers, or soap-makers, or linen merchants, or tavern keepers, or butchers even in the slightest degree. If anyone is found acting contrary to these regulations, he shall be scourged, shorn, and banished.

2. If any victualer has in his possession weights or measures not marked with the seal of the Prefect, or if he pares down gold coins, or if he withdraws from circulation *nomismata* of four or two quarters bearing the genuine imperial stamp, he shall be beaten, shorn, and banished.

3. If a victualer is caught cheating another in a purchase and raising the price agreed upon, he shall be fined ten *nomismata*. Likewise one who exhibits his wares outside his shop on the Lord's Day or on another Holy Day shall undergo the same penalty.

4. The victualers shall keep watch upon the imports that pertain to them, so that, if anyone not enrolled in their gild stores these up against a time of scarcity, he may be denounced to the Prefect and called to account by him.

5. The victualers shall sell their goods in small quantities at a profit of two *miliarisia* on the *nomisma*. If a calculation of their authorized gains shows that they are making a larger profit, they shall be scourged, shorn, and forced to give up this trade.

6. If any one of them secretly or openly raises the rental of another, he shall suffer the aforesaid penalty.

C. The Fury of the People

26. *Procopius,* History of the Wars (*sixth century*): The Nika Riot (532)

Reprinted by permission of the publisher and the Loeb Classical Library from H. B. Dewing, trans., *Procopius* (Cambridge, Mass.: Harvard University Press, 1914), I, 219–39.

. . . [A]n insurrection broke out unexpectedly in Byzantium among the populace, and, contrary to expectation, it proved to be a very serious affair, and ended in great harm to the people and to the senate, as the following account will shew. In every city the population has been divided for a long time past into the Blue and the Green factions; but within comparatively recent times it has come about that, for the sake of these names and the seats which the rival factions occupy in watching the games, they spend their money and abandon their bodies to the most cruel tortures, and even do not think it unworthy to die a most shameful death. And they fight against their opponents knowing not for what end they imperil themselves, but knowing well that, even if they overcome their enemy in the fight, the conclusion of the matter for them will be to be carried off straightway to the prison, and finally, after suffering extreme torture, to be destroyed. So there grows up in them against their fellow men a hostility which has no cause, and at no time does it cease or disappear, for it gives place neither to the ties of marriage nor of relationship nor of friendship, and the case is the same even though those who differ with respect to these colours be brothers or any other kin. They care neither for things divine nor human in comparison with conquering in these struggles; and it matters not whether a sacrilege is committed by anyone at all against God, or whether the laws and the constitution are violated by friend or by foe; nay even when they are perhaps ill supplied with the necessities of life, and when their fatherland is in the most pressing need and suffering unjustly, they pay no heed if only it is likely to go well with their "faction"; for so they name the bands of partisans. And even women join with them in this unholy strife, and they not only follow the men, but even resist them if opportunity offers, although they neither go to the public exhibitions at all, nor are they impelled by any other cause; so that I, for my part, am unable to call this anything except a disease of the soul. This, then, is pretty well how matters stand among the people of each and every city.

But at this time the officers of the city administration in Byzantium were leading away to death some of the rioters. But the members of the two factions, conspiring together and declaring a truce with each other, seized the prisoners and then straightway entered the prison and released all those who were in confinement there, whether they had been condemned on a charge of stirring up sedition, or for any other unlawful act. And all the attendants in the service of the city government were killed indiscriminately; meanwhile, all of the citizens who were sane-minded were fleeing to the opposite mainland, and fire was applied to the city as if it had fallen under the hand of an enemy. The sanctuary of Sophia and the baths of Zeuxippus, and the portion of the imperial residence from the propylaea as far as the so-called House of Ares were destroyed by fire, and besides these both the great colonnades which extended as far as the market place which bears the name of Constantine, in addition to many houses of wealthy men and a vast amount of treasure. During this time the emperor and his consort with a few members of the senate shut themselves up in the palace and remained quietly there. Now the watchword which the populace passed around to one another was Nika, and the insurrection has been called by this name up to the present time.

The praetorian prefect at that time was John the Cappadocian, and Tribunianus, a Pamphylian by birth, was counsellor to the emperor; this person the Romans call "quaestor." One of these two men, John, was entirely without the advantages of a liberal education; for he learned nothing while attending the elementary school except his letters, and these, too, poorly enough; but by his natural ability he became the most powerful man of whom we know. For he was most capable in deciding upon what was needful and in finding a solution for difficulties. But he became the basest of all men and employed his natural power to further his low designs; neither consideration for God nor any shame before man entered into his mind, but to destroy the lives of many men for the sake of gain and to wreck whole cities was his constant concern. So within a short time indeed he had acquired vast sums of money, and he flung himself completely into the sordid life of a drunken scoundrel; for up to the time of lunch each day he would plunder the property of his subjects, and for the rest of the day occupy himself with drinking and with wanton deeds of lust. And he was utterly unable to control himself, for he ate food until he vomited, and he was always ready to steal money and more ready to bring it out and spend it. Such a man then was John. Tribunianus, on the other hand, both possessed natural ability and in educational attainments was inferior to none of his contemporaries; but he was extraordinarily fond of the pursuit of money and always ready to sell justice for gain; therefore every day, as a rule, he was repealing some laws and proposing others, selling off to those who requested it either favour according to their need.

Now as long as the people were waging this war with each other in behalf of the names of the colours, no attention was paid to the offences of these men against the constitution; but when the factions came to a mutual understanding, as has been said, and so began the sedition, then openly throughout the whole city they began to abuse the two and went about seeking them to kill. Accordingly the emperor, wishing to win the people to his side, instantly dismissed both these men from office. And Phocas, a patrician, he appointed praetorian prefect, a man of the greatest discretion and fitted by nature to be a guardian of justice; Basilides he commanded to fill the office of quaestor, a man known among the patricians for his agreeable qualities and a notable besides. However, the insurrection continued no less violently under them. Now on the fifth day of the insurrection in the late afternoon the Emperor Justinian gave orders to Hypatius and Pompeius, nephews of the late emperor, Anastasius, to go home as quickly as possible, either because he suspected that some plot was being matured by them against his own person, or, it may be, because destiny brought them to this. But they feared that the people would force them to the throne (as in fact fell out), and they said that they would be doing wrong if they should abandon their sovereign when he found himself in such danger. When the Emperor Justinian heard this, he inclined still more to his suspicion, and he bade them quit the palace instantly. Thus, then, these two men betook themselves to their homes, and, as long as it was night, they remained there quietly.

But on the following day at sunrise it became known to the people that both men had quit the palace where they had been staying. So the whole population ran to them, and they declared Hypatius emperor and prepared to lead him to the market place to assume the power. But the wife of Hypatius, Mary, a discreet woman, who had the greatest reputation for prudence, laid hold of her husband and would not let go, but cried out with loud lamentation and with entreaties to all her kinsmen that the people were leading him on the road to death. But since the throng overpowered her, she unwillingly released her husband, and he by no will of his own came to the Forum of Constantine, where they summoned him to the throne; then since they had neither diadem nor anything else with which it is customary for a king to be clothed, they placed a golden necklace upon his head and proclaimed him Emperor of the Romans. By this time the members of the senate were assembling,—as many of them as had not been left in the emperor's residence,—and many expressed the opinion that they should go to the palace to fight. But Origenes, a man of the senate, came forward and spoke as follows: "Fellow Romans, it is impossible that the situation which is upon us be solved in any way except by war. Now war and royal power are agreed to be the greatest of all things in the world. But when action involves great issues, it refuses to be brought to a successful conclusion by the brief crisis of a moment, but this is accomplished only by wisdom of thought and energy of action, which men display for a length of time. Therefore if we should go out against the enemy, our cause will hang in the balance, and we shall be taking a risk which will decide everything in a brief space of time; and, as regards the consequences of such action, we shall either fall down and worship Fortune or reproach her altogether. For those things whose issue is most quickly decided, fall, as a rule, under the sway of fortune. But if we handle the present situation more deliberately, not even if we wish shall we be able to take Justinian in the palace, but he will very speedily be thankful if he is allowed to flee; for authority which is ignored always loses its power, since its strength ebbs away with each day. Moreover we have other palaces, both Placillianae and the palace named from Helen, which this emperor should make his headquarters and from there he should carry on the war and attend to the ordering of all other matters in the best possible way." So spoke Origenes. But the rest, as a crowd is accustomed to do, insisted more excitedly and thought that the present moment was opportune, and not least of all Hypatius (for it was fated that evil should befall him) bade them lead the way to the hippodrome. But some say that he came there purposely, being well-disposed toward the emperor.

Now the emperor and his court were deliberating as to whether it would be better for them if they remained or if they took to flight in the ships. And many opinions were expressed favouring either course. And the Empress Theodora also spoke to the following effect: "As to the belief that a woman ought not to be daring among men or to assert herself boldly among those who are holding back from fear, I consider that the present crisis most certainly does not permit us to discuss whether the matter should be regarded in this or in some other way. For in the case of those whose interests have come into the greatest danger nothing else seems best except to settle the issue immediately before them in the best possible way. My opinion then is that the present time, above all others, is inopportune for flight, even though it bring safety. For while it is impossible for a man who has seen the light not also to die, for one who has been an emperor it is unendurable to be a fugitive. May I never be separated from this purple, and may I not live that day on which those who meet me shall not address me as mistress. If, now, it is your wish to save yourself, O Emperor, there is no difficulty. For we have much money, and there is the sea, here the boats. However, consider whether it will not come about after you have been saved that you would gladly exchange that safety for death. For as for myself, I approve a certain ancient saying that royalty is a good burial-shroud." When the queen had spoken thus, all were filled with boldness, and, turning their thoughts towards resistance, they began to consider how they might be able to defend themselves if any hostile force should come against them. Now the soldiers as a body, including those who were stationed about the emperor's court, were neither well-disposed to the emperor nor willing openly to take an active part in fighting, but were waiting for what the future would bring forth. All the hopes of the emperor were centred upon Belisarius and Mundus, of whom the former, Belisarius, had recently returned from the Persian war bringing with him a following which was both powerful and imposing, and in particular he had a great number of spearmen and guards who had received their training in battles and the perils of warfare. Mundus had been appointed general of the Illyrians, and by mere chance had happened to come under summons to Byzantium on some necessary errand, bringing with him Erulian barbarians.

When Hypatius reached the hippodrome, he went up immediately to where the emperor is accustomed to take his place and seated himself on the royal throne from which the emperor was always accustomed to view the equestrian and athletic contests. And from the palace Mundus went out through the gate which, from the circling descent, has been given the name of the Snail. Belisarius meanwhile began at first to go straight up toward Hypatius himself and the royal throne, and when he came to the adjoining structure where there has been a guard of soldiers from of old, he cried out to the soldiers commanding them to open the door for him as quickly as possible, in order that he might go against the tyrant. But since the soldiers had decided to support neither side, until one of them should be manifestly victorious, they pretended not to hear at all and thus put him off. So Belisarius returned to the emperor and declared that the day was lost for them, for the soldiers who guarded the palace were rebelling against him. The emperor therefore commanded him to go to the so-called Bronze Gate and the propylaea there. So Belisarius, with difficulty and not without danger and great exertion, made his way over ground covered by ruins and half-burned buildings, and ascended to the stadium. And when he had reached the Blue Colonnade which is on the right of the emperor's throne, he purposed to go against Hypatius himself first; but since there was a small door there which had been closed and was guarded by the soldiers of Hypatius who were inside, he feared lest while he was struggling in the narrow space the populace should fall upon him, and after destroying both himself and all his followers, should proceed with less trouble and difficulty against the emperor. Concluding, therefore, that he must go against the populace who had taken their stand in the hippodrome—a vast multitude crowding each other in great disorder—he drew his sword from its sheath and, commanding the others to do likewise, with a shout he advanced upon them at a run. But the populace, who were standing in a mass and not in order, at the sight of armoured soldiers who had a great reputation for bravery and experience in war, and seeing that they struck out with their swords unsparingly, beat a hasty retreat. Then a great outcry arose, as was natural, and Mundus, who was standing not far away, was eager to join in the fight,—for he was a daring and energetic fellow—but he was at a loss as to what he should do under the circumstances; when, however, he observed that Belisarius was in the struggle, he straightway made a sally into the hippodrome through the entrance which they call the Gate of Death. Then indeed from both sides the partisans of Hypatius were assailed with might and main and destroyed. When the rout had become complete and there had already been great slaughter of the populace, Boraedes and Justus, nephews of the Emperor Justinian, without anyone daring to lift a hand against them, dragged Hypatius down from the throne, and, leading him in, handed him over together with Pompeius to the emperor. And there perished among the populace on that day more than thirty thousand. But the emperor commanded the two prisoners to be kept in severe confinement. Then while Pompeius was weeping and uttering pitiable words (for the man was wholly inexperienced in such misfortunes), Hypatius reproached him at length and said that those who were about to die unjustly should not lament. For in the beginning they had been forced by the people against their will, and afterwards they had come to the hippodrome with no thought of harming the emperor. And the soldiers killed both of them on the following day and threw their bodies into the sea. The emperor confiscated all their property for the public treasury, and also that of all the other members of the senate who had sided with them. Later, however, he restored to the children of Hypatius and Pompeius and to all others the titles which they had formerly held, and as much of their property as he had not happened to bestow upon his friends. This was the end of the insurrection in Byzantium.

27. *William of Tyre,* History of Deeds Done Beyond the Sea: The Latin Massacre (*1182*)

Reprinted by permission of the publisher from William of Tyre, *A History of Deeds Done Beyond the Sea,* trans. Emily Atwater Babcock and A. C. Krey, Records of Civilization, Sources and Studies (New York: Columbia University Press, 1943), II, 464–65.

The conspiracy continued to gain strength; the *protosebastos* was seized, blinded, and horribly mutilated. This change of affairs spread consternation among the Latins, for they feared that the citizens would make a sudden attack upon them; in fact they had already received warning of such intention from certain people who had private knowledge of the conspiracy. Those who were able to do so, therefore, fled from the wiles of the Greeks and the death which threatened them. Some embarked on forty-four galleys which chanced to be in the harbor, and others placed all their effects on some of the many other ships there.

The aged and infirm, however, with those who were unable to flee, were left in their homes, and on them fell the wicked rage which the others had escaped. For Andronicus, who had secretly caused ships to be prepared, led his entire force into the city. As soon as they entered the gates these troops, aided by the citizens, rushed to that quarter of the city occupied by the Latins and put to the sword the little remnant who had been either unwilling or unable to flee with the others. Although but few of these were able to fight, yet they resisted for a long time and made the enemy's victory a bloody one.

Regardless of treaties and the many services which our people had rendered to the empire, the Greeks seized all those who appeared capable of resistance, set fire to their houses, and speedily reduced the entire quarter to ashes. Women and children, the aged and the sick, all alike perished in the flames. To vent their rage upon secular buildings alone, however, was far from satisfying their unholy wickedness; they also set fire to churches and venerated places of every description and burned, together with the sacred edifices, those who had fled thither for refuge. No distinction was made between clergy and laymen, except that greater fury was displayed toward those who wore the honorable habits of high office or religion. Monks and priests were the especial victims of their madness and were put to death under excruciating torture.

Among these latter was a venerable man named John, a subdeacon of the holy Roman church, whom the pope had sent to Constantinople on business relating to the church. They seized him and, cutting off his head, fastened it to the tail of a filthy dog as an insult to the church. In the midst of such frightful sacrilege, worse than parricide, not even the dead, whom impiety itself generally spares, were suffered to rest undisturbed. Corpses were torn from the tombs and dragged through the streets and squares as if the insensate bodies were capable of feeling the indignities offered them.

The vandals then repaired to the hospital of St. John, as it is called, where they put to the sword all the sick they found. Those whose pious duty it should have been to relieve the oppressed, namely the monks and priests, called in footpads and brigands to carry on the slaughter under promise of reward. Accompanied by these miscreants, they sought out the most secluded retreats and the inmost apartments of homes, that none who were hiding there might escape death. When such were discovered, they were dragged out with violence and handed over to the executioners, who, that they might not work without pay, were given the price of blood for the murder of these wretched victims.

Even those who seemed to show more consideration sold into perpetual slavery among the Turks and other infidels the fugitives who had resorted to them and to whom they had given hope of safety. It is said that more than four thousand Latins of various age, sex, and condition were delivered thus to barbarous nations for a price.

In such fashion did the perfidious Greek nation, a brood of vipers, like a serpent in the bosom or a mouse in the wardrobe evilly requite their guests—those who had not deserved such treatment and were far from anticipating anything of the kind; those to whom they had given their daughters, nieces, and sisters as wives and who, by long living together, had become their friends.

Part Five

BYZANTIUM AND THE WEST

Hostility between Greek-speakers and Latin-speakers went back at least to the fifth century, when popes and emperors had contended about the interpretation of the Creed of Chalcedon. Further religious breaches occurred over the heresies of Monotheletism (seventh century) and Iconoclasm (eighth and ninth centuries), and concerning the disputed patriarchate of Photius (857–867). To disagreements arising out of difficulties of translation were added others regarding divergent religious usages: leavened or unleavened bread in the Lord's Supper, marriage of the clergy (allowed to priests by the Byzantines), the wearing of beards. Photius discovered that the Latins had introduced into the Nicene Creed a statement that the Holy Spirit proceeded from the Father *and from the Son* (*filioque*), whereas the council had mentioned only the Father. The Byzantines thought that this was an incorrect view of the Trinity, and that the Creed should not have been altered without the consent of an ecumenical council.

To reinforce these religious disputes, political rivalry sprang up. The Byzantines could never accept as permanent the loss of Western Europe, especially Italy, and the claim of Charlemagne and his successors to the imperial title was particularly irritating. When Constantine IX Monomachus (1042–1055) (see above, Reading No. 6) tried to oppose the Norman invaders of southern Italy by allying himself with Pope Leo IX, the masterful Patriarch Michael Cerularius opposed the emperor himself. As a result of preliminary misunderstandings, due to the strong characters of the persons involved and to some mistranslations, Pope Leo sent Cardinal Humbert of Silva Candida to Constantinople in 1054. Humbert was as opinionated as Cerularius, and the mild

Constantine IX strove to keep peace between the two. After reading an offensive papal letter (written by Humbert), Cerularius refused to meet the cardinal, and Humbert ended by depositing a papal decree excommunicating the patriarch and his followers on the altar of Haghia Sophia. The emperor tried vainly to mediate the dispute, and Humbert scrupulously avoided condemning him, in hopes that Constantine would side with the papacy against his own patriarch. After his return to Italy, the cardinal composed a short narrative of his actions, incorporating the papal decree. Many of his allegations against the Byzantines were false: for instance, they did not then require rebaptism of Latin Catholics converted to Orthodoxy; the *filioque* issue was only noted in passing. The usage of leavened bread in communion was made the formal grounds for condemnation. Cardinal Humbert's vigorous propaganda caused Westerners to accept his action (Reading No. 28). Thus commenced the schism between Orthodox and Catholic churches.

Medieval contacts between Byzantines and Westerners increased rather than diminished their mutual distaste. Liudprand, Bishop of Cremona, visited Constantinople at least twice, in 949 as representative of an Italian king, and in 968 as ambassador for Otto I, who claimed the title of Roman Emperor in rivalry with the Byzantine Nicephorus II Phocas. Liudprand had enjoyed his first visit, but he was ill-received by Nicephorus, held in Constantinople against his will for half a year, and constrained to watch preparations for war against Otto in Italy. In his report to Otto, a long narrative of his sufferings, he vented his hatred against the pride and perfidy of the Byzantines, and expressed his distaste for their refinements (Reading No. 29).

The crusades did not improve Byzantine-Western relations, though the first one was intended to relieve Turkish pressure against Alexius I (see Reading No. 7), as well as to free the Holy Land. Alexius I wished to welcome the crusaders, but they pillaged his domains on the excuse that Christians owed them support; Alexius was compelled to police the line of march with Petcheneg mercenaries, thereby arousing the crusaders' ire. Similarly, when the Count of Ghent attempted to land his ship south of the usual Adriatic ports, he was met by a Byzantine fleet commanded by Nicholas Maurocatacalon, whose son Marianus played the lead in the resulting encounter. Long afterward, Anna Comnena recorded Marianus' version of the incident, in which a Latin priest distinguished himself by his valor and martial skill. The princess was shocked at such improper and barbarous conduct. At Constantinople, Alexius sought to win the support of the Western leaders by kindness and gifts; their greed and fickleness were already notorious, and Anna Comnena spitefully records the vacillations of Bohemund, son of the Norman Robert Guiscard (Reading No. 30).

The Fourth Crusade (1202–1204) was composed of Frankish knights who believed that the Byzantines had betrayed their predecessors, and Venetians who recollected the Latin Massacre of 1182 (see Reading No. 27) and desired a permanent monopoly of the trade of Constantinople. When a refugee Byzantine prince, Alexius, son of the dethroned Isaac II Angelus, approached the crusaders, offering money and military aid if they would conquer Constantinople for him, they gave him support. In 1203 they won Constantinople, but Alexius found it impossible to fulfill his promises, and conflict broke out again. In 1204 the crusaders seized the city for themselves, and subjected it to three days of rape and plundering. The Byzantines never forgot this terrible event; in 1207 a witness, the rhetorician Nicholas Mesarites, recorded his memories (Reading No. 31). Not until 1261 did the Byzantines regain their capital, and the empire was never restored to its former greatness. The Byzantines could not forget that, while engaged in conflict with the infidel, they had been stabbed in the back by their fellow Christians. Attempts to heal the breach were made, but all foundered on deeply rooted Byzantine hostility to Latins.

A. The Breach of 1054

28. *Humbert, Cardinal of Silva Candida*

J.-P. Migne, ed., *Patrologiae Cursus Completus . . . Series Latina,* CXLIII (Paris, 1882), 1001–4. Translated by the editor.

Brief and Concise Memorandum of what the envoys of the holy Roman and apostolic see did in the royal city, and how Michael with his followers were anathematized.

In the eleventh year of the reign of Constantine Monomachus, Indiction VII, on the very day of the nativity of the blessed John the Baptist [June 24, 1054] the envoys of the holy Roman see from the Lord Pope Leo IX, to wit Humbert, cardinal-bishop of Silva Candida, Peter, Archbishop of Amalfi, and Frederick, the deacon and chancellor [later Pope Stephen IX], arrived at the Monastery of Studius within the city of Constantinople. . . .

While Michael [Cerularius] avoided the presence and converse of these same [envoys] and continued in his folly, the said envoys, defeated by his obstinacy, entered the church of Haghia Sophia on July 16 at the third hour [ca. 9 A.M.] of the Sabbath when the clergy customarily was ready for the liturgy, and placed the text of an excommunication on the chief altar under the eyes of the attendant clergy and people. Quickly departing thence, they also shook the dust from their feet in witness to them, crying out the phrase of the Gospel: May God see and judge.[1] Hence when the churches of the Latins within Constantinople had been regulated and an anathema pronounced on all who thereafter received communion from the hand of a Greek who disparaged the Roman Eucharist, permission of the orthodox emperor having been received in the kiss of peace and with imperial gifts for [the see of] St. Peter and themselves, on July 18 they commenced speedily to return. But the emperor, forced by the excessive pressure of Michael's requests, since the latter then vowed that he would contend with them, summoned them back from Selymbria [southwest of Constantinople] by his letters on July 20. Hastening on the same day they returned to the palace of Pege. When the aforesaid heretic-leader Michael learned that they had returned, he attempted to bring them to a synod in Haghia Sophia on the following day, so that when the document [the excommunication], which he had totally falsified in translation, was produced, they might be overwhelmed there by the people. The wise emperor, guarding against this, was unwilling to hold any synod unless he himself was present. And since Michael entirely forbade him this, the emperor commanded the envoys speedily to take up their journey, which they did. Further the frantic Michael, grieving that his traps had not succeeded, aroused a great crowd of people against the emperor, since his goodwill had supported the legates. The emperor, compelled thereby, turned over to Michael the interpre-

[1] Unidentified.

tors of the Latins, Paul and his son Smaragdus, who were lopped and tonsured, and thus quieted the tumult. But the emperor received by his men whom he dispatched after the Roman legates a very exact copy of the excommunication sent back from the city of Rossa [Rhesium, north of Gallipoli], and showed it to the citizens, and so disclosed and demonstrated that Michael had forged the decree of the legates. Thus aroused, he expelled his [Michael's] friends and connections, deprived of their honors, from the palace, and still harbors severe anger against him. Finally, here is a copy of the excommunication decree:

"Humbert, by grace of God cardinal-bishop of the holy Roman church; Peter, Archbishop of Amalfi; Frederick, deacon and chancellor: to all sons of the Catholic Church.

"The holy Roman and first apostolic see, to whom as to a head belongs a special care for all churches, for the sake of ecclesiastical peace and profit has deigned to make us its messengers to this royal city, so that, as is written, we might descend and see whether in fact the outcry resounds which continuously arises from that city to its [the Roman see's] ears, or if this is not so, to know it. Wherefore before everything [else] the glorious emperors, the clergy, the senate, and the people of this city of Constantinople and the whole Catholic Church should learn that we here perceived a great good, whereat we rejoiced mightily in the Lord, and a very great evil, whereat we were pitifully saddened. For in what pertains to the pillars of empire and its honored wise citizens, the city is most Christian and orthodox. Yet as to Michael miscalled patriarch and the supporters of his folly, they daily sow abundant tares of heresy in its midst. Whereas like Simoniacs they sell God's gift; like Valesians they castrate their serfs and not only promote them into the clergy but even to the episcopate; like Arians they rebaptize those baptized in the name of the holy Trinity, and especially Latins; like Donatists they declare that, the Greeks' church excepted, the church of Christ and true communion and baptism have vanished from the whole world; like the Nicolaites they allow and maintain carnal marriage for servants of the sacred altar [priests]; like the Severians they call the law of Moses accursed; like the enemies of the Holy Spirit or enemies of God [fourth-century heretics] they remove from the Creed the procession of the Holy Spirit from the Son; like the Manichaeans among other things, they consider anything fermented to be alive; like the Nazarenes they maintain the fleshly purity of the Jews so far that they forbid infants who die before the eighth day from their birth to be baptized, and forbid women in menstruation or endangered in childbirth to take communion or, if they are pagan, to be baptized, and being people who cultivate the hair of head and beard they do not receive in communion those who cut their hair and shave their beards according to the teachings of the Roman church. This Michael having been admonished by the letter of our lord Pope Leo for these errors and his many other acts disdained to come to his senses. In addition he denied his presence and converse to us his [Leo's] envoys, who wished by reasoning to check the occasion of so many evils, and refused [us] churches for saying masses, just as he had previously closed the churches of the Latins [in Constantinople], and calling them Azymites [i.e., users of unleavened bread in the Eucharist] he persecuted them everywhere by words and deeds, in so much that he has cursed the apostolic see in the persons of its sons, [and] in opposition to it he still writes himself as ecumenical [universal] patriarch. Wherefore we, not enduring the unheard-of abuse and injury of the holy first apostolic see, and considering the Catholic faith to be corrupted in many ways, by the authority of the holy and undivided Trinity and of the apostolic see whose legation we perform and of all the orthodox Fathers of the seven councils and of the whole Catholic Church thus subscribe to the anathema which our most reverend pope pronounced alike on Michael and his followers, unless they regained their senses, as follows:

"Let Michael the neophyte, miscalled patriarch, who attained the garb of monks out of human fear alone, and who is now also defamed for most wicked crimes, and with him Leo called Bishop of Ochrida and his treasurer Michael, [and] Constantine who trampled with profane feet the Eucharist of the Latins and all their followers in the aforesaid errors and audacities, be Anathema Maranatha,[2] with the Simoniacs, Vallesians, Arians, Donatists, Nicolaites, Severians, enemies of the Holy Spirit, and Manichaeans, and Nazarenes, and with all heretics, nay rather with the devil and his angels, unless perchance they recover their senses. Amen, amen, amen."

Likewise another excommunication was orally made there in the presence of the emperor and his nobles:

"Let whoever has stubbornly opposed the faith of the holy Roman and apostolic see and its Eucharist be Anathema Maranatha, and let him not be considered a Catholic Christian but a Prozymite ["leavened bread"] heretic. Be it so, be it so, be it so."

[2] See I Cor. 16:22.

B. Suspicion and Hatred

29. *Liudprand of Cremona,* The Embassy to Constantinople (*968*)

From *The Works of Liudprand of Cremona,* trans. F. A. Wright (New York, 1930), pp. 236–37, 240–43, 251, 263–64, 267–69. Published by E. P. Dutton & Co., Inc., and reprinted with their permission, and with permission of Routledge & Kegan Paul Ltd., London.

On the seventh of June, the sacred day of Pentecost, I was brought before Nicephorus himself in the palace called Stephana, that is, the Crown Palace. He is a monstrosity of a man, a dwarf, fat-headed and with tiny mole's eyes; disfigured by a short, broad, thick beard half going gray; disgraced by a neck scarcely an inch long; piglike by reason of the big close bristles on his head; in colour an Ethiopian and, as the poet says, "you would not like to meet him in the dark"; a big belly, a lean posterior, very long in the hip considering his short stature, small legs, fair sized heels and feet; dressed in a robe made of fine linen, but old, foul smelling, and discoloured by age; shod with Sicyonian slippers; bold of tongue, a fox by nature, in perjury and falsehood a Ulysses. . . .

As Nicephorus, like some crawling monster, walked along, the singers began to cry out in adulation: "Behold the morning star approaches: the day star rises: in his eyes the sun's rays are reflected: Nicephorus our prince, the pale death of the Saracens." And then they cried again: "Long life, long life to our prince Nicephorus. Adore him, ye nations, worship him, bow the neck to his greatness." How much more truly might they have sung:—"Come, you miserable burnt-out coal; old woman in your walk, wood-devil in your look; clodhopper, haunter of byres, goat-footed, horned, double-limbed; bristly, wild, rough, barbarian, harsh, hairy, a rebel, a Cappadocian!" . . .

On this same day he ordered me to be his guest. But as he did not think me worthy to be placed above any of his nobles, I sat fifteenth from him and without a table cloth. Not only did no one of my suite sit at table with me; they did not even set eyes upon the house where I was entertained. At the dinner, which was fairly foul and disgusting, washed down with oil after the fashion of drunkards and moistened also with an exceedingly bad fish liquor, the emperor asked me many questions concerning your power, your dominions and your army. My answers were sober and truthful; but he shouted out:—"You lie. Your master's soldiers cannot ride and they do not know how to fight on foot. The size of their shields, the weight of their cuirasses, the length of their swords, and the heaviness of their helmets, does not allow them to fight either way." Then with a smile he added: "Their gluttony also prevents them. Their God is their belly, their courage but wind, their bravery drunkenness. Fasting for them means dissolution, sobriety, panic. Nor has your master any force of ships on the sea. I alone have really stout sailors, and I will attack him with my fleets, destroy his maritime cities and reduce to ashes those which have a river near them. Tell me, how with his small forces will he be able to resist me even on land? His son was there: his wife was there: his Saxons, Swabians, Bavarians and Italians were all there with him: and yet they had not the skill nor the strength to take one little city that resisted them. How then will they resist me when I come followed by as many forces as there are

> Corn fields on Gargarus, grapes on Lesbian vine,
> Waves in the ocean, stars in heaven that shine?"

I wanted to answer and make such a speech in our defence as his boasting deserved; but he would not let me and added this final insult: "You are not Romans but Lombards." He even then was anxious to say more and waved his hand to secure my silence, but I was worked up and cried: "History tells us that Romulus, from whom the Romans get their name, was a fratricide born in adultery. He made a place of refuge for himself and received into it insolvent debtors, runaway slaves, murderers and men who deserved death for their crimes. This was the sort of crowd whom he enrolled as citizens and gave them the name of Romans. From this nobility are descended those men whom you style 'rulers of the world.' But we Lombards, Saxons,

Franks, Lotharingians, Bavarians, Swabians and Burgundians so despise these fellows that when we are angry with an enemy we can find nothing more insulting to say than—'You Roman!' For us in the word Roman is comprehended every form of lowness, timidity, avarice, luxury, falsehood and vice. You say that we are unwarlike and know nothing of horsemanship. Well, if the sins of the Christians merit that you keep this stiff neck, the next war will prove what manner of men you are, and how warlike we." . . .

I was anxious to go away, but he ordered me to return to his table. His father sat with him, a man, it seemed to me, a hundred and fifty years old. For him, as for his son, the Greeks cry out in hymns of praise, or rather of blatant folly, "May God multiply your years." We may infer from this how senseless the Greeks are, how fond of such windy talk, how apt at flattery, and how greedy. Not merely is he an old man, but he has one foot in the grave; and yet they pray for him something that they know for certain nature will not allow. The old tombstone himself rejoices that they are asking on his behalf for what he knows God will not grant, something that, if God did grant it, would be a curse, and not a blessing. Nicephorus, for his part, takes pleasure in being hailed as "Prince of Peace" and "Morning Star." To call a weakling strong, a fool wise, a pygmy a giant, a black man white, a sinner a saint, is not praise, believe me, but contumely. And he who takes more pleasure in false attributes than in real is exactly like those birds whose sight is blinded by the light of day and illumined by the shades of night. . . .

To increase my calamities, on the day of the Assumption of the Virgin Mary the holy mother of God, an ill-omened embassy came from the apostolic and universal Pope John with a letter asking Nicephorus "the emperor of the Greeks" to conclude an alliance and firm friendship with his beloved and spiritual son Otto, "august emperor of the Romans." If you ask me why these words, and manner of address, which to the Greeks seem sinful audacity, did not cost the bearer his life and overwhelm it even before they were read, I cannot answer. On other points I have often shown a fine and copious flow of words; on this I am as dumb as a fish. The Greeks abused the sea, cursed the waves, and wondered exceedingly how they could have transported such an iniquity, and why the deep had not opened to swallow up the ship. "The audacity of it!" they cried, "to call the universal emperor of the Romans, the one and only Nicephorus, the great, the august 'emperor of the Greeks,' and to style a poor barbaric creature 'emperor of the Romans'! O sky! O earth! O sea! What shall we do with these scoundrels and criminals? They are paupers, and if we kill them we pollute our hands with vile blood; they are ragged, they are slaves, they are peasants; if we beat them we disgrace not them but ourselves; they are not worthy of our gilded Roman scourge, or of any punishment of that kind. Would that one of them were a bishop and the other a marquess! Then we would sew them in a sack, and after giving them a sound beating with rods and plucking out their beards and hair we would throw them into the sea. As for these fellows, their lives may be spared; but they shall be kept in close custody until Nicephorus, the sacred emperor of the Romans, be informed of these insults." . . .

". . . And since we think that you have bought some cloaks in his honour, we order them now to be produced. Those that are fit for you shall be marked with a leaden seal and left in your possession; those that are prohibited to all nations, except to us Romans, shall be taken away and their price returned."

Thereupon they took from me five very valuable pieces of purple cloth; considering yourselves and all the Italians, Saxons, Franks, Bavarians, Swabians—nay, all nations—as unworthy to appear abroad in such ornate vestments. How improper and insulting is it that these soft, effeminate creatures, with their long sleeves and hoods and bonnets, idle liars of neither gender, should go about in purple, while heroes like yourselves, men of courage, skilled in war, full of faith and love, submissive to God, full of virtues, may not! "But where is your emperor's word?" I said. "Where is the imperial promise? When I said farewell to him, I asked him up to what price he would allow me to buy vestments in honour of my church. He replied, 'Buy any that you like and as many as you like.' In thus fixing quality and quantity he clearly did not make a distinction, as if he had said, 'excepting this and that.' His brother Leo, the marshal of the palace, can bear me witness; so can the interpreter Euodisius, and John and Romanus. I can testify to it myself, for even without the interpreter I understood what the emperor said." "But these stuffs are prohibited," they replied, "and when the emperor spoke as you say he did he could not imagine that you would ever dream of such things as these. As we surpass all other nations in wealth and wisdom, so it is right that we should surpass them in dress. Those who are unique in the grace of their virtue should also be unique in the beauty of their raiment."

"Such garments can hardly be called unique," I said, "when with us street walkers and conjurors wear them." "Where do you get them from?" they asked. "From Venetian and Amalfian traders," I replied, "who by bringing them to us support life by the food we give them." "They shall not do so any longer," they answered. "They shall be searched, and if any cloth of this kind be found on them, they shall be punished with a beating and have their hair clipped close." "In the time of the Emperor Constantine, of blessed memory," I said, "I came here not as bishop but as deacon, not sent by an emperor or king but by the Marquess Berengar. I then bought many more vestments of greater value than those I have bought now, and they were not inspected, and scrutinised by the Greeks, nor yet stamped with a leaden seal. Now, having become a bishop by the mercy of God and being sent as envoy by the magnificent emperors, Otto and Otto, father and son, I am treated with ignominy; my vestments are marked after the manner of the Venetians, and any of them that seem of value are taken from me, although they are being transported for use in the church entrusted to my care. Are you not weary of insulting me, or rather, my masters, for whose sake I am thus scorned? Is it not enough that I was given into custody, tortured by hunger and thirst, and not allowed to return to them, but detained here until now? Must you also, as one final insult to them, rob me of things that are honestly mine? At least only take away what I purchased; leave me what was presented as a gift by friends." To that they replied: "The emperor Constantine was a mild man, who always stayed in his palace, and by peaceful methods won the friendship of all the world. The Emperor Nicephorus on the other hand shuns the palace as if it were the plague. We call him a man of contention and almost a lover of strife; he does not win people's friendship by offering them money, he subdues them to his sway by terror and the sword. And that you may realise in what esteem we hold your royal masters, we shall treat gifts and purchases in the same way: every purple vestment you have acquired must be returned to us."

30. *Anna Comnena,* Alexiad

Reprinted by permission of the publishers, Routledge & Kegan Paul Ltd., London, and Barnes & Noble, Inc., New York, from Anna Comnena, *The Alexiad of the Princess Anna Comnena,* trans. Elizabeth A. S. Dawes (London: Kegan Paul, Trench, Trubner & Co., Ltd., 1928), pp. 248, 250, 256–57, 266.

Before he had enjoyed even a short rest, he heard a report of the approach of innumerable Frankish armies. Now he dreaded their arrival for he knew their irresistible manner of attack, their unstable and mobile character and all the peculiar natural and concomitant characteristics which the Frank retains throughout; and he also knew that they were always agape for money, and seemed to disregard their truces readily for any reason that cropped up. For he had always heard this reported of them, and found it very true. However, he did not lose heart, but prepared himself in every way so that, when the occasion called, he would be ready for battle. . . .

According to universal rumour Godfrey, who had sold his country, was the first to start on the appointed road; this man was very rich and very proud of his bravery, courage and conspicuous lineage; for every Frank is anxious to outdo the others. And such an upheaval of both men and women took place then as had never occurred within human memory, the simpler-minded were urged on by the real desire of worshipping at our Lord's Sepulchre, and visiting the sacred places; but the more astute, especially men like Bohemund and those of like mind, had another secret reason, namely, the hope that while on their travels they might by some means be able to seize the capital itself, looking upon this as a kind of corollary. And Bohemund disturbed the minds of many nobler men by thus cherishing his old grudge against the Emperor. . . .

A certain Latin priest who happened to be standing in the stern with twelve other fighting men, saw this [that Marianus had been hit in the arm] and let fly several arrows against Marianus. Not even then did Marianus surrender, but fought fiercely himself and encouraged his men to do the same, so that three times over the men with the priest had to be replaced, as they were wounded and sore-pressed. The priest himself, however, although he had received many blows, and was streaming with his own blood, remained quite fearless. For the rules concerning priests are not the same among the Latins as they are with us; for we are given the command by the canonical laws and the teaching of the Gospel, "Touch not, taste not, handle not! For thou art consecrated." Whereas the Latin barbarian will simultaneously handle divine things, and wear his shield on his left arm, and hold his spear in his right hand, and at one and the same time he communicates the body and blood of God, and looks murderously and becomes "a man of blood," as it says in the psalm of David. For this barbarian race is no less devoted to sacred things than it is to war. And so this man of violence rather than priest, wore his priestly garb at the same time that he handled the oar and had an eye equally to naval or land warfare, fighting simultaneously with the sea and with men. But our rules, as I have just remarked, are derived from the . . . of Aaron and Moses and our first high-priest. After the battle had raged fiercely from the evening till next midday, the Latins surrendered to Marianus, much against their will, after asking and obtaining a promise of immunity.

But that most bellicose priest did not stop fighting, even while the truce was being concluded, but as he had emptied his quiver of darts, he picked up a sling-stone and hurled it at Marianus. The latter protected his head with his shield, but the stone struck the shield and broke it in four pieces and shattered his helmet. And Marianus was overwhelmed by the blow from the stone, and at once fell unconscious, and lay speechless a long time, just as the hero Hector almost gave up the ghost when hit with a stone by Ajax. He recovered with difficulty, and then pulled himself together and by shooting arrows at him, thrice hit the man who had struck him. Yet that polemarch, rather than priest, was not even then sated with fighting, and as he had hurled all the stones he had, he was now utterly unarmed and bereft both of stones and of darts; so not knowing what to do or how to defend himself against his adversary, he grew impatient, and stormed and raged and twisted himself about like a wild beast; and directly he saw anything handy he used it. Then he discovered a sack of barley-cakes and began throwing out the barley-cakes from the sack as though they were stones, as if he were officiating and taking a service, and turning war into a sacred celebration. And one barley-cake he picked up, drove it with all his might, aiming at Marianus' face, and hit him on the cheek. So much for that priest and the ship and its crew. The Count of

Prebentza, after surrendering himself and his ship and his soldiers to Marianus, immediately followed him. And when they had reached land and were disembarking, that same priest often and repeatedly asked for Marianus and, because he did not know his name, he called him by the colour of his clothes. When he found him, he threw his arms round him and embraced him, whilst saying boastfully, "If you had met me on dry land, many of you would have been killed by my hands." Then he pulled out and gave him a large silver cup worth one hundred and thirty staters. And with these words and this gift he breathed his last. . . .

The Emperor sent for Bohemund and requested him to take the customary oath of the Latins. And he, mindful of his own position, namely, that he was not descended from illustrious ancestors, nor had a great supply of money, and for this reason not even many troops, but only a very limited number of Frankish retainers, and being moreover by nature ready to swear falsely, yielded readily to the Emperor's wish. Then the Emperor selected a room in the palace and had the floor strewn with every kind of riches, . . . and so filled the chamber with garments and stamped gold and silver, and other materials of lesser value, that one could not even walk because of their quantity. And he told the man who was to show Bohemund these things, to throw open the doors suddenly. Bohemund was amazed at the sight and exclaimed, "If all these treasures were mine, I should have made myself master of many countries long ere this!" and the attendant replied, "The Emperor makes you a present of all these riches to-day." Bohemund was overjoyed and after thanking for the present he went away to rest in the house where he lodged. But when these treasures were brought to him, he who had admired them before had changed his mind and said, "Never did I imagine that the Emperor would inflict such dishonour on me. Take them away and give them back to him who sent them." But the Emperor, knowing the Latins' characteristic fickleness, quoted the popular proverb, "Let bad things return to their own master." When Bohemund heard of this and saw the porters carefully packing the presents up again, he changed his mind—he, who a minute before was sending them away and was annoyed at them, now gave the porters pleasant looks, just like a polypus that changes its form in an instant. For by nature the man was a rogue and ready for any eventualities; in roguery and courage he was far superior to all the Latins who came through then, as he was inferior to them in forces and money.

But in spite of his surpassing all in superabundant activity in mischief, yet fickleness like some natural Latin appendage attended him too. So he who first rejected the presents, afterwards accepted them with great pleasure.

C. The Sack of Constantinople, 1204

31. *Nicholas Mesarites,* Funeral Oration

Nicholas Mesarites, "Epitaphius," translated by the editor. Reprinted by permission of the publisher from Charles M. Brand, *Byzantium Confronts the West, 1180–1204* (Cambridge, Mass.: Harvard University Press, 1968), p. 269.

Then the streets, squares, two-storied and three-storied houses, holy places, convents, houses of monks and nuns, holy churches (even God's Great Church), the imperial palace, were filled with the enemy, all war-maddened swordsmen, breathing murder, iron-clad and spear-bearing, sword-bearers and lance-bearers, bowmen, horsemen, boasting dreadfully, baying like Cerberus and breathing like Charon, pillaging the holy places, trampling on divine things, running riot over holy things, casting down to the floor the holy images (on walls or on panels) of Christ and His holy Mother and of the holy men who from eternity have been pleasing to the Lord God, uttering calumnies and profanities, and in addition tearing children from mothers and mothers from children, treating the virgin with wanton shame in holy chapels, viewing with fear neither the wrath of God nor the vengeance of men. Breasts of women were searched [to see] whether a feminine ornament or gold was fastened to the body or hidden in them, hair was unloosed and head-coverings removed, and the homeless and moneyless were dragged to the ground. Lamentation, moan and woe were everywhere. Indecency was perpetrated, if any fair object was concealed within the recesses of the body; thus the ill-doers and mischief-makers abused nature itself. They slaughtered the newborn, killed prudent [matrons], stripped elder women, and outraged old ladies; they tortured the monks, they hit them with their fists and kicked their bellies, thrashing and rending their reverend bodies with whips. Mortal blood was spilled on the holy altars, and on each, in place of the Lamb of God sacrificed for the salvation of the universe, many were dragged like sheep and beheaded, and on the holy tombs the wretches slew the innocent. Such was the reverence for holy things of those who bore the Lord's Cross on their shoulders, thus their own bishops taught them to act. . . .

Part Six

ISLAMIC CIVILIZATION

While the Byzantine Empire struggled to survive, a new Arab civilization arose, founded on the teachings of the Prophet Mohammed (A.D. 570–632). Mohammed, who grew up in the trading city of Mecca in western Arabia, had encountered Jews and Christians; some of his doctrines came from them. But he himself believed that the Angel Gabriel had appeared to him and revealed divine messages for the instruction of the pagan Arabs. His teachings stressed the singleness, unity, and power of God and the approach of the judgment day. The individual should accept this faith (the very name "Islam" signifies "submission"), pray regularly, give alms, fast during the holy month of Ramadan, and if possible make a pilgrimage to Mecca. Mohammed's words were written down by his followers as "Surahs" or Chapters; after his death these were put together in the Koran, the sacred book of Islam. Except for the opening prayer, the Surahs were arranged in order of length, longest first, so that many of Mohammed's earliest statements occur in the latter part of the volume. The opening verses of Surah XCVI are said to have been the first revealed; other texts expound the unity and greatness of God, his beneficence as Creator, the delights of Paradise and pains of Hell, and the duties of Moslems (Reading No. 32). Mohammed spoke as the Spirit guided him, and the reader must not hope for a logical exposition; further, his followers sometimes added to the confusion by combining revelations from different periods in the same Surah.

At Mohammed's death, he was spiritual and military leader of much of Arabia, and his successors expanded into Palestine, Syria, Mesopotamia, Persia, Egypt, and ultimately to Spain and the borders of China. The religious development of Islam did not cease with the passing of the Prophet. To supplement the Koran, a body of traditions regarding alleged sayings and actions of Mohammed grew up. Groups of individuals seeking to lead truly religious lives withdrew from the world to practice asceticism; they believed that the purified soul could enter into contact with God Himself. The teachings of these Sufis, gradually accepted by conservative Moslem intellectuals, were integrated with Koranic theology in the writings of al-Ghazzali (1058–1111) (Reading No. 33).

Their conquests opened to the Arabs the world of Greek thought. Interest in medicine and astrology sent students to such Hellenistic handbooks as Galen's great compilation on medical science. From these they pushed back to the sources of Greek knowledge, especially Aristotle. Among the pioneer scholars was Abú Becr Mohammed ibn Zacaríyá ar-Rází, called by medieval Westerners Rhazes (864–925); the opening chapter of his "Treatise on the Small-Pox and Measles" displays his high regard for Galen. He accepted the theory that bodily health was based on a balance of the four humors (liquids) of the body: blood, phlegm, yellow bile, and black bile. Smallpox he therefore attributed to a change in the quality of blood (Reading No. 34).

The study of Aristotle's scientific writings led to interest in his philosophy, and Arab and Persian thinkers eagerly seized on his concepts of the universe. Among the greatest of Islamic thinkers was the Persian Abu Ali al-Husain ibn Abd Allah, called Ibn Sina, and known to Westerners as Avicenna (980–1037). He came from Bokhara in northeastern Persia (now in Soviet Central Asia), which in his youth was a flourishing cultural center; in his *Autobiography* he records how he mastered the whole field of knowledge, especially Greek science and philosophy. His demonstration of the existence of God was strongly influenced by Aristotle (Reading No. 35). Such a rationalist approach challenged the revealed doctrines of Islam, and al-Ghazzali set himself to reply. A sketch of the lengthy refutations he had previously published is included in his *Confessions* (Reading No. 36). Al-Ghazzali was successful; only in Spain did an Aristotelian approach survive until the death of Averroes in 1198.

Although philosophy was forbidden, some other sciences still flourished. The wide extent of the Moslem world and the practice of pilgrimage encouraged the writing of travel accounts and geographies. Utilizing these and stimulated by his own experience in government service, the Tunisian Abd-ar-Rahman ibn Khaldun, Abu Zayd (1332–1406), composed his *Muqaddimah* (an introduction to his universal history), in which he formulated social, political, and historical theories. Mankind, ibn Khaldun believed, was divided into townsmen and Bedouins (in which term he included nomadic herdsmen and back-country farmers). Townsmen were bearers of culture and the institutions of organized society, but Bedouins were superior in such virtues as courage and endurance. Further, the Bedouins possessed a strong sense of tribal unity or "group feeling," which tended to break down in an urban environment. Thus, from time to time, Bedouin tribes would conquer areas of urban culture where virtue and group feeling had waned. The victors would found a new dynasty, but would in time suffer moral and political decay, as luxury spread and scions of the ruling house contended with one another. Then a new wave of invaders would sweep over the land. Such revolutions would recur indefinitely and similar cycles prevailed in cultural history. Ibn Khaldun's work forms the culmination of medieval Islamic thought, and many of his theories anticipate doctrines of modern sociology (Reading No. 37).

A. Religious Foundations

32. *The Koran*

The Koran (Qur'ân), trans. E. H. Palmer, The World's Classics (London: Oxford University Press, 1928), pp. 1, 36, 373–77, 436–40, 466–69, 530–32, 537.

The Chapter of Congealed Blood
XCVI (*Mecca*)

In the name of the merciful and compassionate God.

Read, in the name of thy Lord!

Who created man from congealed blood!
Read, for thy Lord is most generous!
[5] Who taught the pen!
Taught man what he did not know!
Nay, verily, man is indeed outrageous at seeing himself get rich!
Verily, unto thy Lord is the return!
Hast thou considered him who forbids [10] a servant when he prays?
Hast thou considered if he were in guidance or bade piety?
Hast thou considered if he said it was a lie and turned his back?
Did he not know that God can see?
[15] Nay, surely, if he do not desist we will drag him by the fore-lock!—the lying sinful forelock!
So let him call his counsel: we will call the guards of hell!
Nay, obey him not, but adore and draw nigh!

THE CHAPTER OF UNITY
CXII (*Place of origin doubtful*)

In the name of the merciful and compassionate God.

Say, "He is God alone!
God the Eternal!
He begets not and is not begotten!
Nor is there like unto Him any one!"

THE CHAPTER OF THE HEIFER
II:256 (*Medina*)
"THE THRONE-VERSE"

God, there is no god but He, the living, the self-subsistent. Slumber takes Him not, nor sleep. His is what is in the heavens and what is in the earth. Who is it that intercedes with Him save by His permission? He knows what is before them and what behind them, and they comprehend not aught of His knowledge but of what He pleases. His throne extends over the heavens and the earth, and it tires Him not to guard them both, for He is high and grand.

The Opening Chapter
I (*Mecca*)

In the name of the merciful and compassionate God.

Praise *belongs* to God, the Lord of the worlds, the merciful, the compassionate, the ruler of the day of judgment! Thee we serve and Thee we ask for aid. [5] Guide us in the right path, the path of those Thou art gracious to; not of those Thou art wroth with; nor of those who err.

The Chapter of the Manifest Sign
XCVIII (*Place of origin doubtful*)

In the name of the merciful and compassionate God.

Those of the people of the Book and the idolaters who misbelieve did not fall off until there came to them the manifest sign,—

An apostle from God reading pure pages wherein are right scriptures:

Nor did those who were given the Book divide into sects until after there came to them the manifest sign.

But they were not bidden aught but to worship God, being sincere in religion unto Him as ʿHanîfs, and to be steadfast in prayer, and to give alms: for that is the standard religion.

[5] Verily, those who disbelieve amongst the people of the Book and the idolaters shall be in the fire of hell, to dwell therein for aye; they are wretched creatures!

Verily, those who believe and act aright, they are the best of creatures; their reward with their Lord is gardens of Eden, beneath which rivers flow, to dwell therein for aye; God shall be well pleased with them, and they with Him! that is for him who fears his Lord!

The Chapter of the Inevitable
LVI (*Mecca*)

In the name of the merciful and compassionate God.

When the inevitable happens; none shall call its happening a lie!—abasing—exalting!

When the earth shall quake, quaking! [5] and the mountains shall crumble, crumbling, and become like motes dispersed!
And ye shall be three sorts;
And the fellows of the right hand—what right lucky fellows!
And the fellows of the left hand—what unlucky fellows!
[10] And the foremost foremost!
These are they who are brought nigh,
In gardens of pleasure!
A crowd of those of yore,
And a few of those of the latter day!
[15] And gold-weft couches, reclining on them face to face.
Around them shall go eternal youths, with goblets and ewers and a cup of flowing wine; no headache shall they feel therefrom, nor shall their wits be dimmed!
[20] And fruits such as they deem the best;
And flesh of fowl as they desire;
And bright and large-eyed maids like hidden pearls;
A reward for that which they have done!
They shall hear no folly there and no sin;
[25] Only the speech, "Peace, Peace!"
And the fellows of the right—what right lucky fellows!
Amid thornless lote trees.
And talʿh trees with piles of fruit;
And outspread shade,
[30] And water out-poured;
And fruit in abundance, neither failing nor forbidden;
And beds upraised!
Verily, we have produced them a production.
[35] And made them virgins, darlings of equal age (with their spouses) for the fellows of the right!
A crowd of those of yore, and a crowd of those of the latter day!
[40] And the fellows of the left—what unlucky fellows!
In hot blasts and boiling water;
And a shade of pitchy smoke,
Neither cool nor generous!
Verily, they were affluent ere this, [45] and did persist in mighty crime; and used to say, "What, when we die and have become dust and bones, shall we then indeed be raised? or our fathers of yore?"

Say, "Verily, those of yore and those of the latter day [50] shall surely be gathered together unto the tryst of the well-known day."

Then ye, O ye who err! who say it is a lie! shall eat of the Zaqqûm tree! and fill your bellies with it! and drink thereon of boiling water! [55] and drink as drinks the thirsty camel.

This is their entertainment on the judgment day!

We created you, then why do ye not credit?

Have ye considered what ye emit?

Do ye create it, or are we the creators?

[60] We have decreed amongst you death; but we are not forestalled from making the likes of you in exchange, or producing you as ye know not of.

Ye do know the first production—why then do ye not mind?

Have ye considered what ye till?

Do ye make it bear seed, or do we make it bear seed?

[65] If we pleased we could make it mere grit, so that ye would pause to marvel:

"Verily, we have got into debt and we are excluded."

Have ye considered the water which ye drink?

Do ye make it come down from the clouds, or do we make it come down?

If we pleased we could make it pungent—why then do ye not give thanks?

[70] Have ye considered the fire which ye strike?

Do ye produce the tree that gives it, or do we produce it?

We have made it a memorial and a chattel for the traveller of the waste!

Then celebrate the grand name of thy Lord!

So I will not swear by the positions of the stars; [75] and, verily, it is a grand oath if ye did but know—that, verily, this is the honourable Qur'ân—in the laid-up Book!

Let none touch it but the purified!

A revelation from the Lord of the worlds.

[80] What! this new discourse will ye despise?

And make for your provision, that you call it a lie?

Why then—when it comes up to the throat, and ye at that time look on, though we are nearer to him than you are, but ye cannot see,—[85] why, if ye are not to be judged, do ye not send it back, if ye do tell the truth?

But either, if he be of those brought nigh to God,—then rest and fragrance and the garden of pleasure!
Or, if he be of the fellows of the right! [90] then "Peace to thee!" from the fellows of the right!
Or, if he be of those who say it is a lie,—who err! then an entertainment of boiling water! and broiling in hell!
[95] Verily, this is surely certain truth!
So celebrate the grand name of thy Lord!

The Chapter of the Angels
XXXV (*Mecca*)

In the name of the merciful and compassionate God.

Praise belongs to God, the originator of the heavens and the earth; who makes the angels His messengers, endued with wings in pairs, or threes or fours; He adds to creation what He pleases; verily, God is mighty over all!

What God opens to men of His mercy there is none to withhold; and what He withholds, there is none can send it forth after Him; for He is the mighty, the wise.

O ye folk! remember the favours of God towards you; is there a creator beside God, who provides you from the heavens and from the earth? There is no god but He; how then can ye lie?

And if they call thee liar, apostles were called liars before thee, and unto God affairs return.

[5] O ye folk! verily, God's promise is true; then let not the life of this world beguile you, and let not the beguiler beguile you concerning God. Verily, the devil is to you a foe, so take him as a foe; he only calls his crew to be the fellows of the blaze.

Those who misbelieve, for them is keen torment.

But those who believe and do right, for them is forgiveness and a great hire.

What! is he whose evil act is made seemly for him, so that he looks upon it as good,———? Verily, God leads astray whom He pleases and guides whom He pleases; let not thy soul then be wasted in sighing for them; verily, God knows what they do!

[10] It is God who sends the winds, and they stir up a cloud, and we

irrigate therewith a dead country, and we quicken therewith the earth after its death; so shall the resurrection be!

Whosoever desires honour—honour belongs wholly to God; to Him good words ascend, and a righteous deed He takes up; and those who plot evil deeds, for them is keen torment, and their plotting is in vain.

God created you from earth, then from a clot; then He made you pairs; and no female bears or is delivered, except by His knowledge; nor does he who is aged reach old age, or is aught diminished from his life, without it is in the Book; verily, that is easy unto God.

The two seas are not equal: one is sweet and fresh and pleasant to drink, and the other is salt and pungent; but from each do ye eat fresh flesh, and bring forth ornaments which ye wear; and thou mayest see the ships cleave through it, that ye may search after His grace, and haply ye may give thanks.

He turns the night into day, and He turns the day into night; and He subjects the sun and the moon, each of them runs on to an appointed goal; that is God, your Lord! His is the kingdom; but those ye call on beside Him possess not a straw.

[15] If you call upon them they cannot hear your call, and if they hear they cannot answer you; and on the resurrection day they will deny your associating them with God; but none can inform thee like the One who is aware.

O ye folk! ye are in need of God; but God, He is independent, praiseworthy.

If He please He will take you off, and will bring a fresh creation; for that is no hard matter unto God.

And no burdened soul shall bear the burden of another; and if a heavily laden one shall call for its load (to be carried) it shall not be carried for it at all, even though it be a kinsman!—thou canst only warn those who fear their Lord in the unseen and who are steadfast in prayer; and he who is pure is only pure for himself; and unto God the journey is.

[20] The blind is not equal with him who sees, nor the darkness with the night, nor the shade with the hot blast; nor are the living equal with the dead; verily, God causes whom he pleases to hear, and thou canst not make those who are in their graves hear; thou art but a warner!

Verily, we have sent thee in truth a herald of glad tidings and a warner; and there is no nation but its warner has passed away with it.

And if they called thee liar, those before thee called their apostles liars too, who came to them with manifest signs, and the Scriptures, and the illuminating Book.

Then I seized those who misbelieved, and what a change it was!

[25] Dost thou not see that God has sent down from the heaven water, and has brought forth therewith fruits varied in hue, and on the mountains dykes, white and red, various in hue, and some intensely black, and men and beasts and cattle, various in hue? thus! none fear God but the wise among His servants; but, verily, God is mighty, forgiving.

Verily, those who recite the Book of God, and are steadfast in prayer, and give alms of what we have bestowed in secret and in public, hope for the merchandise that shall not come to naught; that He may pay them their hire, and give them increase of His grace; verily, He is forgiving, grateful.

What we have inspired thee with of the Book is true, verifying what was before it; verily, God of His servants is well aware and sees.

Then we gave the Book for an inheritance to those whom we chose of our servants, and of them are some who wrong themselves, and of them are some who take a middle course, and of them are some who vie in good works by the permission of their Lord; that is great grace.

[30] Gardens of Eden shall they enter, adorned therein with bracelets of gold and pearls; and their garments therein shall be silk; and they shall say, "Praise belongs to God, who has removed from us our grief; verily, our Lord is forgiving, grateful! who has made us alight in an enduring abode of His grace, wherein no toil shall touch us, and there shall touch us no fatigue."

But those who misbelieve, for them is the fire of hell; it shall not be decreed for them to die, nor shall aught of the torment be lightened from them; thus do we reward every misbeliever; and they shall shriek therein, "O our Lord! bring us forth, and we will do right, not what we used to do!"—"Did we not let you grow old enough for every one who would be mindful to be mindful? and there came to you a warner!—[35] So taste it, for the unjust shall have none to help!" verily, God knows the unseen things of the heavens and of the earth; verily, He knows the nature of men's breasts, He it is who made you vicegerents in the earth, and he who misbelieves, his misbelief is against himself;

but their misbelief shall only increase the misbelievers in hatred with their Lord; and their misbelief shall only increase the misbelievers in loss.

Say, "Have ye considered your associates whom ye call on beside God?" show me what they created of the earth; have they a share in the heavens, or have we given them a book that they rest on a manifest sign? nay, the unjust promise each other naught but guile.

Verily, God holds back the heavens and the earth lest they should decline; and if they should decline there is none to hold them back after Him; verily, He is clement, forgiving.

[40] They swore by God with their most strenuous oath, verily, if there come to them a warner they would be more guided than any one of the nations; but when a warner comes to them, it only increases them in aversion, and in being big with pride in the earth, and in plotting evil; but the plotting of evil only entangles those who practise it; can they then expect aught but the course of those of yore? but thou shalt not find any alteration in the course of God; and they shall not find any change in the course of God.

Have they not journeyed on in the land and seen what was the end of those before them who were stronger than they? but God, nothing can ever make Him helpless in the heavens or in the earth; verily, He is knowing, powerful.

Were God to catch men up for what they earn, He would not leave upon the back of it a beast; but He respites them until an appointed time. [45] When their appointed time comes, verily, God looks upon His servants.

The Chapter of Mohammed, Also Called Fight
XLVII (*Medînah*)

In the name of the merciful and compassionate God.

Those who misbelieve and turn folk from God's way, He will make their works go wrong. But those who believe and do right and believe in what is revealed to Mohammed,—and it is the truth from their Lord—He will cover for them their offences and set right their mind.

That is because those who misbelieve follow falsehood, and those who believe follow the truth from their Lord. Thus does God set forth for men their parables.

And when ye meet those who misbelieve—then striking off heads until ye have massacred them, and bind fast the bonds!

[5] Then either a free grant (of liberty) or a ransom until the war shall have laid down its burdens. That!—but if God please He would conquer them—but (it is) that He may try some of you by the others. And those who are slain in God's cause, their works shall not go wrong; He will guide them and set right their mind; and will make them enter into Paradise which He has told them of.

O ye who believe! if ye help God, He will help you, and will make firm your footsteps.

But as for those who misbelieve—confound them! and He will make their works go wrong.

[10] That is because they were averse from what God has revealed; but their works shall be void!

Have they not journeyed through the land and seen how was the end of those before them? God destroyed them; and for the misbelievers is the like thereof.

That is because God is the patron of those who believe, and because the misbelievers have no patron.

Verily, God causes those who believe and do right to enter into gardens beneath which rivers flow; but those who misbelieve enjoy themselves and eat as the cattle eat; but the fire is the resort for them!

How many a city, stronger than thy city which has driven thee out, have we destroyed, and there was none to help them!

[15] Is he who rests upon a manifest sign from his Lord like him, the evil of whose works is made seemly to him, and who follow their lusts?

The similitude of Paradise which is promised to the pious,—in it are rivers of water without corruption, and rivers of milk, the taste whereof changes not, and rivers of wine delicious to those who drink; and rivers of honey clarified; and there shall they have all kinds of fruit and forgiveness from their Lord! [Is that] like him who dwells in the fire for aye? and who are given to drink boiling water that shall rend their bowels asunder?

Some of them there are who listen to thee, until when they go forth from thee they say to those who have been given the knowledge, "What is this which he says now?" These are those on whose hearts God has set a stamp and who follow their lusts.

But those who are guided, He guides them the more, and gives them the due of their piety.

[20] Do they wait for aught but the Hour, that it should come to them suddenly? The conditions thereof have come already; how, when it has come on them, can they have their reminder?

Know thou that there is no god but God; and ask pardon for thy sin and for the believers, men and women; for God knows your return and your resort!

Those who misbelieve say, "Why has not a sûrah been revealed?" but when a decisive sûrah is revealed and fighting is mentioned therein, thou mayest see those in whose heart is sickness looking towards thee with the look of one fainting in death. Preferable for them were obedience and a reasonable speech! But when the matter is determined on, then if they believed God it were better for them.

Would ye perhaps, if ye had turned back, have done evil in the land and severed the bonds of kinship?

[25] It is these whom God has cursed, and has made them deaf, and has blinded their eyesight! Do they not peruse the Qurʾân? or are there locks upon their hearts?

Verily, those who turn their backs after the guidance that has been manifested to them—Satan induces them, but [God] lets them go on for a time!

That is for that they say to those who are averse from what God has revealed, "We will obey you in part of the affair!" but God knows their secrets! How will it be when the angels take their souls, smiting their faces and their backs?

[30] This is because they follow what angers God and are averse from His goodwill; and their works are void.

Do those in whose hearts is sickness reckon that God will not bring their malice forth?

But did we please we would show thee them, and thou shouldst know them by their cognisances. But thou shalt know them by their distorting their speech, and God knows their works!

But we will try you until we know those among you who fight strenuously and the patient; and we will try the reports concerning you.

Verily, those who misbelieve and turn folks off God's path, and break with the Apostle after the guidance that has been manifested to them, cannot harm God at all, and their works shall be void!

[35] O ye who believe! obey God, and obey the Apostle; and make not your works vain.

Verily, those who misbelieve and turn folks off God's path, and then die misbelievers, God will not pardon them.

Then faint not, nor cry for peace while ye have the upper hand; for God is with you and will not cheat you of your works!

The life of this world is but a play and a sport; but if ye believe and fear God, He will give you your hire.

He does not ask you for [all] your property; if He were to ask you for it and to press you, ye would be niggardly, and he would bring your malice out.

[40] Here are ye called upon to expend in God's cause, and among you are some who are niggardly; and he who is niggardly is but niggardly against his own soul: but God is rich and ye are poor, and if ye turn your backs He will substitute another people in your stead, then they will not be like you.

33. *Al-Ghazzali (1058–1111)*, Alchemy of Happiness

Reprinted by permission of the publisher from Al-Ghazzali, *The Alchemy of Happiness,* trans. Claud Field, The Wisdom of the East Series (London: John Murray [Publishers] Ltd., 1910), pp. 23–24, 51–54, 100–4, 106–8.

Now the rational soul in man abounds in marvels, both of knowledge and power. By means of it he masters arts and sciences, can pass in a flash from earth to heaven and back again, can map out the skies and measure the distances between the stars. By it also he can draw the fish from the sea and the birds from the air, and can subdue to his service animals like the elephant, the camel, and the horse. His five senses are like five doors opening on the external world; but, more wonderful than this, his heart has a window which opens on the unseen world of spirits. In the state of sleep, when the avenues of the senses are closed, this window is opened and man receives impressions from the unseen world and sometimes foreshadowings of the future. His heart is then like a mirror which reflects what is pictured in the

Tablet of Fate. But, even in sleep, thoughts of worldly things dull this mirror, so that the impressions it receives are not clear. After death, however, such thoughts vanish and things are seen in their naked reality, and the saying in the Koran is fulfilled: "We have stripped the veil from off thee and thy sight to-day is keen."

This opening of a window in the heart towards the unseen also takes place in conditions approaching those of prophetic inspiration, when intuitions spring up in the mind unconveyed through any sense-channel. The more a man purifies himself from fleshly lusts and concentrates his mind on God, the more conscious will he be of such intuitions. Those who are not conscious of them have no right to deny their reality. . . .

As regards the joys of heaven and the pains of hell which will follow this life, all believers in the Koran and the Traditions are sufficiently informed. But it often escapes them that there is also a spiritual heaven and hell, concerning the former of which God said to His Prophet, "Eye hath not seen, nor ear heard, neither hath it entered into the heart of man to conceive the things which are prepared for the righteous." In the heart of the enlightened man there is a window opening on the realities of the spiritual world, so that he knows, not by hearsay or traditional belief, but by actual experience, what produces wretchedness or happiness in the soul just as clearly and decidedly as the physician knows what produces sickness or health in the body. He recognises that knowledge of God and worship are medicinal, and that ignorance and sin are deadly poisons for the soul. Many even so-called "learned" men, from blindly following others' opinions, have no real certainty in their beliefs regarding the happiness or misery of souls in the next world, but he who will attend to the matter with a mind unbiassed by prejudice will arrive at clear convictions on this matter.

The effect of death on the composite nature of man is as follows: Man has two souls, an animal soul and a spiritual soul, which latter is of angelic nature. The seat of the animal soul is the heart, from which this soul issues like a subtle vapour and pervades all the members of the body, giving the power of sight to the eye, the power of hearing to the ear, and to every member the faculty of performing its own appropriate functions. It may be compared to a lamp carried about within a cottage, the light of which falls upon the walls wherever it goes. The heart is the wick of this lamp, and when the supply of oil is cut off for any reason, the lamp dies. Such is the death of the animal soul. With the spiritual, or human soul, the case is different. It is indivisible, and by it man knows God. It is, so to speak, the rider of the animal soul, and when that perishes it still remains, but is like a horseman who has been dismounted, or like a hunter who has lost his weapons. That steed and those weapons were granted the human soul that by means of them it might pursue and capture the Phœnix of the love and knowledge of God. If it *has* effected that capture, it is not a grief but rather a relief to be able to lay those weapons aside, and to dismount from that weary steed. Therefore the Prophet said, "Death is a welcome gift of God to the believer." But alas for that soul which loses its steed and hunting-weapons before it has captured the prize! Its misery and regret will be indescribable.

A little further consideration will show how entirely distinct the human soul is from the body and its members. Limb after limb may be paralysed and cease working, but the individuality of the soul is unimpaired. Further, the body which you have now is no longer the body which you had as a child, but entirely different, yet your Personality now is identical with your personality then. It is therefore easy to conceive of it as persisting when the body is done with altogether, along with its essential attributes which were independent of the body, such as the knowledge and love of God. This is the meaning of that saying of the Koran, "The good things abide." But if, instead of carrying away with you knowledge, you depart in ignorance of God, this ignorance also is an essential attribute, and will abide as darkness of soul and the seed of misery. Therefore the Koran says, "He who is blind in this life will be blind in the next life, and astray from the path."

The reason of the human spirit seeking to return to that upper world is that its origin was from thence, and that it is of angelic nature. It was sent down into this lower sphere against its will to acquire knowledge and experience, as God said in the Koran: "Go down from hence, all of you; there will come to you instruction from Me, and they who obey the instruction need not fear, neither shall they be grieved." The verse, "I breathed into man of My spirit," also points to the celestial origin of the human soul. Just as the health of the animal soul consists in the equilibrium of its component parts, and this equilibrium is restored, when impaired, by appropriate medicine, so the health of the human soul consists in a moral equilibrium which is maintained and repaired, when needful, by ethical instruction and moral precepts. . . .

The love of God is the highest of all topics, and is the final aim to which we have been tending hitherto. We have spoken of spiritual dangers as they hinder the love of God in a man's heart, and we have spoken of various good qualities as being the necessary preliminaries to it. Human perfection resides in this, that the love of God should conquer a man's heart and possess it wholly, and even if it does not possess it wholly it should predominate in the heart over the love of all other things. Nevertheless, rightly to understand the love of God is so difficult a matter that one sect of theologians have altogther denied that man can love a Being who is not of his own species, and they have defined the love of God as consisting merely in obedience. Those who hold such views do not know what real religion is.

All Moslems are agreed that the love of God is a duty. God says concerning the believers, "He loves them and they love Him," and the Prophet said, "Till a man loves God and His Prophet more than anything else he has not the right faith." When the angel of death came to take the soul of Abraham the latter said, "Have you ever seen a friend take his friend's life?" God answered him, "Have you ever seen a friend unwilling to see his friend?" Then Abraham said, "O Azrael! take my soul!" The following prayer was taught by the Prophet to his companions, "O God, grant me to love Thee and to love those who love Thee, and whatsoever brings me nearer to Thy love, and make Thy love more precious to me than cold water to the thirsty." Hassan Basri used to say, "He who knows God loves Him, and he who knows the world hates it."

We come now to treat of love in its essential nature. Love may be defined as an inclination to that which is pleasant. This is apparent in the case of the five senses, each of which may be said to love that which gives it delight; thus the eye loves beautiful forms, the ear music, etc. This is a kind of love we share with the animals. But there is a sixth sense, or faculty of perception, implanted in the heart, which animals do not possess, through which we become aware of spiritual beauty and excellence. Thus, a man who is only acquainted with sensuous delights cannot understand what the Prophet meant when he said he loved prayer more than perfumes or women, though the last two were also pleasant to him. But he whose inner eye is opened to behold the beauty and perfection of God will despise all outward sights in comparison, however fair they may be.

The former kind of man will say that beauty resides in red-and-white complexions, well-proportioned limbs, and so forth, but he will be blind to moral beauty, such as men refer to when they speak of such and such a man as possessing a "beautiful" character. But those possessed of inner perception find it quite possible to love the departed great, such as the Caliphs Omar and Abu Bakr, on account of their noble qualities, though their bodies have long been mingled with the dust. Such love is directed not towards any outward form, but towards the inner character. Even when we wish to excite love in a child towards any one, we do not describe their outward beauty of form, etc., but their inner excellencies.

When we apply this principle to the love of God we shall find that He alone is really worthy of our love, and that, if any one loves Him not, it is because he does not know Him. Whatever we love in any one we love because it is a reflection of Him. It is for this reason that we love Muhammad, because he is the Prophet and the Beloved of God, and the love of learned and pious men is really the love of God. We shall see this more clearly if we consider what are the causes which excite love.

The first cause is this, that man loves himself and the perfection of his own nature. This leads him directly to the love of God, for man's very existence and man's attributes are nothing else but the gift of God, but for whose grace and kindness man would never have emerged from behind the curtain of non-existence into the visible world. Man's preservation and eventual attainment to perfection are also entirely dependent upon the grace of God. It would indeed be a wonder, if one should take refuge from the heat of the sun under the shadow of a tree and not be grateful to the tree, without which there would be no shadow at all. Precisely in the same way, were it not for God, man would have no existence nor attributes at all; wherefore, then, should he not love God, unless he be ignorant of Him? Doubtless fools cannot love Him, for the love of Him springs directly from the knowledge of Him, and whence should a fool have knowledge?

The second cause of this love is that man loves his benefactor, and in truth his only Benefactor is God, for whatever kindness he receives from any fellow-creature is due to the immediate instigation of God.

Whatever motive may have prompted the kindness he receives from another, whether the desire to gain religious merit or a good name, God is the Agent who set that motive to work.

The third cause is the love that is aroused by contemplation of the attributes of God, His power and wisdom, of which human power and wisdom are but the feeblest reflections. This love is akin to that we feel to the great and good men of the past, such as the Imam Malik and the Imam Shafi, though we never expect to receive any personal benefits from them, and is therefore a more disinterested kind of love. God said to the prophet David, "That servant is dearest to Me who does not seek Me from fear of punishment or hope of reward, but to pay the debt due to My Deity." And in the Psalms it is written, "Who is a greater transgressor than he who worships Me from fear of hell or hope of heaven? If I had created neither, should I not then have deserved to be worshipped?"

The fourth cause of this love is the affinity between man and God, which is referred to in the saying of the Prophet, "Verily God created man in His own likeness." Furthermore, God has said, "My servant seeks proximity to Me, that I may make him My friend, and when I have made him My friend I become his ear, his eye, his tongue." Again, God said to Moses, "I was sick, and thou didst not visit Me?" Moses replied, "O God! Thou art Lord of heaven and earth: how couldest Thou be sick?" God said, "A certain servant of Mine was sick; hadst thou visited him, thou wouldst have visited Me." . . .

The truth of the matter is this, that, just as the seed of man becomes a man, and a buried date-stone becomes a palm-tree, so the knowledge of God acquired on earth will in the next world change into the Vision of God, and he who has never learnt the knowledge will never have the Vision. This Vision will not be shared alike by all who know, but their discernment of it will vary exactly as their knowledge. God is one, but He will be seen in many different ways, just as one object is reflected in different ways by different mirrors, some showing it straight, and some distorted, some clearly and some dimly. A mirror may be so crooked as to make even a beautiful form appear misshapen, and a man may carry into the next world a heart so dark and distorted that the sight which will be a source of peace and joy to others will be to him a source of misery. He, in whose heart the love of God has prevailed over all else, will derive more joy from this vision than he in whose heart it has not so prevailed; just as in the case of two men with equally powerful eyesight, gazing on a beautiful face, he who already loves the possessor of that face will rejoice in beholding it more than he who does not. For perfect happiness mere knowledge is not enough, unaccompanied by love, and the love of God cannot take possession of a man's heart till it be purified from love of the world, which purification can only be effected by abstinence and austerity. While he is in this world a man's condition with regard to the Vision of God is like that of a lover who should see his Beloved's face in the twilight, while his clothes are infested with hornets and scorpions, which continually torment him. But should the sun arise and reveal his Beloved's face in all its beauty, and the noxious vermin leave off molesting him, then the lover's joy will be like that of God's servant, who, released from the twilight and the tormenting trials of this world, beholds Him without a veil. Abu Suleiman said, "He who is busy with himself now will be busy with himself then, and he who is occupied with God now will be occupied with Him then."

B. Intellectual Development

34. *Rhazes (864–925)*, Treatise on the Small-Pox and Measles

Rhazes (i.e., Abú Becr Mohammed ibn Zacaríyá ar-Rází), *A Treatise on Small-Pox and Measles,* trans. William A. Greenhill (London, 1848), pp. 27–31.

OF THE CAUSES OF THE SMALL-POX; HOW IT COMES TO PASS THAT HARDLY ANY ONE ESCAPES THE DISEASE; AND THE SUM OF WHAT GALEN SAYS CONCERNING IT.

As to any physician who says that the excellent Galen has made no mention of the Small-Pox, and was entirely ignorant of this disease, surely he must be one of those who have either never read his works at all, or who have passed over them very cursorily. For Galen describes a plaster in the first book of his treatise κατὰ γένος, and says that it is useful against this and that disease, "and also against the *Small-Pox*." Again, in the beginning of the fourteenth book of his treatise "On Pulses," at about the first leaf, he says, that "the blood is sometimes putrefied in an extraordinary degree, and that the excess of inflammation runs so high that the skin is burned, and there break out in it the *Small-Pox* and excoriating erysipelas by which it is eroded." Again, in the ninth book of his treatise "On the Use of the Members," he says that "the superfluous parts of the food that remain, which are not converted into blood, and remain in the members, putrefy, and become more acid, in process of time, until there are generated the erysipelas, *Small-Pox,* and spreading inflammation." Again, in the fourth book of "Timaeus" he says that "the ancients applied the name φλεγμονή to every thing in which there was inflammation, as the erysipelas, and *Small-Pox,* and that these diseases were in their opinion generated from bile."

(2.) If, however, any one says that Galen has not mentioned any peculiar and satisfactory mode of treatment for this disease, nor any complete cause, he is certainly correct; for, unless he has done so in some of his works which have not been published in Arabic, he has made no further mention of it than what we have just cited. As for my own part, I have most carefully inquired of those who use both the Syriac and Greek languages, and have asked them about this matter; but there was not one of them who could add anything to what I have mentioned; and indeed most of them did not know what he meant by those passages which I have distinctly quoted. This I was much surprised at, and also how it was that Galen passed over this disease which occurs so frequently and requires such careful treatment, when he is so eager in finding out the causes and treatment of other maladies.

(3.) As to the moderns, although they have certainly made some mention of the treatment of the Small-Pox, (but without much accuracy and distinctness,) yet there is not one of them who has mentioned the cause of the existence of the disease, and how it comes to pass that hardly any one escapes it, or who has disposed the modes of treatment in their right places. And for this reason we hope that the reward of that man who encouraged us to compose this treatise, and also our own, will be doubled, since we have mentioned whatever is necessary for the treatment of this disease, and have arranged and carefully disposed every thing in its right place, by GOD's permission.

(4.) We will now begin therefore by mentioning the efficient cause of this distemper, and why hardly any one escapes it; and then we will treat of the other things that relate to it, section by section: and we will (with GOD's assistance,) speak on every one of these points with what we consider to be sufficient copiousness.

(5.) I say then that every man, from the time of his birth till he arrives at old age, is continually tending to dryness; and for this reason the blood of children and infants is much moister than the blood of young men, and still more so than that of old men. And besides this it is much hotter; as Galen testifies in his Commentary on the "Aphorisms," in which he says that "the heat of children is greater in quantity than the heat of young men, and the heat of young men is more intense in quality." And this also is evident from the force with which the natural processes, such as digestion and growth of body, are carried on in children. For this reason the blood of infants and children may be compared to must, in which the coction leading to perfect ripeness has not yet begun, nor the movement towards fermentation taken place; the blood of young men may be compared to must, which has already fermented and made a hissing noise, and has thrown out abundant vapours and its superfluous parts, like wine which is now still and quiet and arrived at its full strength; and as to the blood of old men, it may be compared to wine which has now lost its strength and is beginning to grow vapid and sour.

(6.) Now the Small-Pox arises when the blood putrefies and ferments, so that the superfluous vapours are thrown out of it, and it is changed from the blood of infants, which is like must, into the blood of young men, which is like wine perfectly ripened: and the Small-Pox itself may be compared to the fermentation and the hissing noise which take place in must at that time. And this is the reason why children, especially males, rarely escape being seized with this disease, because it is impossible to prevent the blood's changing from this state into its second state, just as it is impossible to prevent must (whose nature it is to make a hissing noise and to ferment) from changing into the state which happens to it after its making a hissing noise and its fermentation. And the temperament of an infant or child is seldom such that it is possible for its blood to be changed from the first state into the second by little and little, and orderly, and slowly, so that this fermentation and hissing noise should not show itself in the blood:

for a temperament, to change thus gradually, should be cold and dry; whereas that of children is just the contrary, as is also their diet, seeing that the food of infants consists of milk; and as for children, although their food does not consist of milk, yet it is nearer to it than is that of other ages; there is also a greater mixture in their food, and more movement after it; for which reason it is seldom that a child escapes this disease. Then afterwards alterations take place in their condition according to their temperaments, regimen, and natural disposition, the air that surrounds them, and the state of the vascular system both as to quantity and quality, for in some individuals the blood flows quickly, in others slowly, in some it is abundant, in others deficient, in some it is very bad in quality, in others less deteriorated.

(7.) As to young men, whereas their blood is already passed into the second state, its maturation is established, and the superfluous particles of moisture which necessarily cause putrefaction are now exhaled; hence it follows that this disease only happens to a few individuals among them, that is, to those whose vascular system abounds with too much moisture, or is corrupt in quality with a violent inflammation; or who in their childhood have had the Chicken-Pox, whereby the transition of the blood from the first into the second state has not been perfected. It takes place also in those who have a slight heat, or whose moisture is not copious; and to those who had the Chicken-Pox in their childhood, and are of a dry, lean habit of body, with slight and gentle heat; and who when they became young men, used a diet to strengthen and fatten their body, or a diet which corrupted their blood.

(8.) And as for old men, the Small-Pox seldom happens to them, except in pestilential, putrid, and malignant constitutions of the air, in which this disease is chiefly prevalent. For a putrid air, which has an undue proportion of heat and moisture, and also an inflamed air, promotes the eruption of this disease, by converting the spirit in the two ventricles of the heart to its own temperament, and then by means of the heart converting the whole of the blood in the arteries into a state of corruption like itself.

Having thus sufficiently, though briefly and succinctly, treated of the causes of the Small-Pox, we shall now proceed to speak of the habits of body which are most disposed to this disease and to the Measles.

35. *Avicenna (960–1037)*, "Autobiography" *and* "On the Nature of God"

Reprinted by permission of the publisher from Arthur J. Arberry, trans., *Avicenna on Theology,* The Wisdom of the East Series (London: John Murray [Publishers] Ltd., 1951), pp. 9–13, 25–33.

Autobiography of Avicenna.

My father was a man of Balkh, and he moved from there to Bukhara during the days of Nūḥ ibn Manṣūr; in his reign he was employed in the administration, being governor of a village-centre in the outlying district of Bukhara called Kharmaithan. Near by is a village named Afshana, and there my father married my mother and took up his residence; I was also born there, and after me my brother. Later we moved to Bukhara, where I was put under teachers of the Koran and of letters. By the time I was ten I had mastered the Koran and a great deal of literature, so that I was marvelled at for my aptitude.

Now my father was one of those who had responded to the Egyptian propagandist (who was an Ismaili); he, and my brother too, had listened to what they had to say about the Spirit and the Intellect, after the fashion in which they preach and understand the matter. They would therefore discuss these things together, while I listened and comprehended all that they said; but my spirit would not assent to their argument. Presently they began to invite me to join the movement, rolling on their tongues talk about philosophy, geometry, Indian arithmetic; and my father sent me to a certain vegetable-seller who used the Indian arithmetic, so that I might learn it from him. Then there came to Bukhara a man called Abū ʿAbd Allāh al-Nātilī who claimed to be a philosopher; my father invited him to stay in our house, hoping that I would learn from him also. Before his advent I had already occupied myself with Muslim jurisprudence, attending Ismāʿīl the Ascetic; so I was an excellent enquirer, having become familiar with the methods of postulation and the techniques of rebuttal according to the usages of the canon lawyers. I now commenced reading the *Isagoge* (of Porphyry) with al-Nātilī: when he mentioned to me the definition of *genus* as a term applied to a number of things of different species in answer to the question "What is it?" I set about verifying this definition in a manner such as he had never heard. He marvelled at me exceedingly, and warned my father that I should not engage in any other occupation but learning; whatever problem he stated to me, I showed a better mental conception of it than he. So I continued until I had read all the straightforward parts of Logic with him; as for the subtler points, he had no acquaintance with them.

From then onward I took to reading texts by myself; I studied the commentaries, until I had completely mastered the science of Logic. Similarly with Euclid I read the first five or six figures with him, and thereafter undertook on my own account to solve the entire remainder of the book. Next I moved on to the *Almagest* (of Ptolemy); when I had finished the prolegomena and reached the geometrical figures, al-Nātilī told me to go on reading and to solve the problems by myself; I should merely revise what I read with him, so that he might indicate to me what was right and what was wrong. The truth is that he did not really teach this book; I began to solve the work, and many were the complicated figures of which he had no knowledge until I presented them to him, and made him understand them. Then al-Nātilī took leave of me, setting out for Gurganj.

I now occupied myself with mastering the various texts and commentaries on natural science and metaphysics, until all the gates of knowledge were open to me. Next I desired to study medicine, and proceeded to read all the books that have been written on this subject. Medicine is not a difficult science, and naturally I excelled in it in a very short time, so that qualified physicians began to read medicine with me. I also undertook to treat the sick, and methods of treatment derived from practical experience revealed themselves to me such as baffle description. At the same time I continued between whiles to study and dispute on law, being now sixteen years of age.

The next eighteen months I devoted entirely to reading; I studied Logic once again, and all the parts of philosophy. During all this time I did not sleep one night through, nor devoted my attention to any other matter by day. I prepared a set of files; with each proof I examined, I set down the syllogistic premisses and put them in order in the files, then I examined what deductions might be drawn from them. I observed methodically the conditions of the premisses, and proceeded until the truth of each particular problem was confirmed for me. Whenever I found myself perplexed by a problem, or could not find the middle term in any syllogism, I would repair to the mosque and pray, adoring the All-Creator, until my puzzle was resolved and my difficulty made easy. At night I would return home, set the lamp before me, and busy myself with reading and writing; whenever sleep overcame me or I was conscious of some weakness, I turned aside to drink a glass of wine until my strength returned to me; then I went back to my reading. If ever the least slumber overtook me, I would dream of the precise problem which I was considering as I fell asleep; in that way many problems revealed themselves to me while sleeping. So I continued until I had made myself master of all the sciences; I now comprehended them to the limits of human possibility. All that I learned during that time is exactly as I know it now; I have added nothing more to my knowledge to this day.

I was now a master of Logic, natural sciences and mathematics. I therefore returned to metaphysics; I read the *Metaphysica* [of Aristotle], but did not understand its contents and was baffled by the author's intention; I read it over forty times, until I had the text by heart. Even then I did not understand it or what the author meant, and I despaired within myself, saying, "This is a book which there is no way of understanding." But one day at noon I chanced to be in the booksellers' quarter, and a broker was there with a volume in his hand which he was calling for sale. He offered it to me, but I returned it to him impatiently, believing that there was no use in this particular science. However he said to me, "Buy this book from me: it is cheap, and I will sell it to you for four dirhams. The owner is in need of the money." So I bought it, and found that it was a book by Abū Naṣr al-Fārābī *On the Objects of the Metaphysica*. I returned home and hastened to read it; and at once the objects of that book [i.e., Aristotle's *Metaphysica*] became clear to me, for I had it all by heart. I rejoiced at this, and upon the next day distributed much in alms to the poor in gratitude to Almighty God.

Now the Sultan of Bukhara at that time was Nūḥ ibn Manṣūr, and it happened that he fell sick of a malady which baffled all the physicians. My name was famous among them because of the breadth of my reading; they therefore mentioned me in his presence, and begged him to summon me. I attended the sick-room, and collaborated with them in treating the royal patient. So I came to be enrolled in his service. One day I asked his leave to enter their library, to examine the contents and read the books on medicine; he granted my request, and I entered a mansion with many chambers, each chamber having chests of books piled one upon another. In one apartment were books on language and poetry, in another law, and so on; each apartment was set aside for books on a single science. I glanced through the catalogue of the works of the ancient Greeks, and asked for those which I required; and I saw books whose very names are as yet unknown to many—works which I had never seen before and have not seen since. I read these books, taking notes of their contents; I came to realize the place each man occupied in his particular science.

So by the time I reached my eighteenth year I had exhausted all these sciences. My memory for learning was at that period of my life better than it is now, but to-day I am more mature; apart from this my knowledge is exactly the same, nothing further having been added to my store since then. . . .

On the Nature of God

That there is a necessary being

Whatever has being must either have a reason for its being, or have no reason for it. If it has a reason, then it is contingent, equally before it comes into being (if we make this mental hypothesis) and when it is in the state of being—for in the case of a thing whose being is contingent the mere fact of its entering upon being does not remove from it the contingent nature of its being. If on the other hand it has no reason for its being in any way whatsoever, then it is necessary in its being. This rule having been confirmed, I shall now proceed to prove that there is in being a being which has no reason for its being.

Such a being is either contingent or necessary. If it is necessary, then the point we sought to prove is established. If on the other hand it is contingent, that which is contingent cannot enter upon being except for some reason which sways the scales in favour of its being and against its not-being. If the reason is also contingent, there is then a chain of contingents linked one to the other, and there is no being at all; for this being which is the subject of our hypothesis cannot enter into being so long as it is not preceded by an infinite succession of beings, which is absurd. Therefore contingent beings end in a Necessary Being.

Of the unicity of God

It is not possible in any way that the Necessary Being should be two. Demonstration: Let us suppose that there is another necessary being: one must be distinguishable from the other, so that the terms "this" and "that" may be used with reference to them. This distinction must be either essential or accidental. If the distinction between them is accidental, this accidental element cannot but be present in each of them, or in one and not the other. If each of them has an accidental element by which it is distinguished from the other, both of them must be caused; for an accident is what is adjoined to a thing after its essence is realized. If the accidental element is regarded as adhering to its being, and is present in one of the two and not in the other, then the one which has no accidental element is a necessary being and the other is not a necessary being. If, however, the distinction is essential, the element of essentiality is that whereby the essence as such subsists; and if this element of essentiality is different in each and the two are distinguishable by virtue of it, then each of the two must be a compound; and compounds are caused; so that neither of them will be a necessary being. If the element of essentiality belongs to one only, and the other is one in every respect and there is no compounding of any kind in it, then the one which has no element of essentiality is a necessary being, and the other is not a necessary being. Since it is thus established that the Necessary Being cannot be two, but is All Truth, then by virtue of His Essential Reality, in respect of which He is a Truth, He is United and One, and no other shares with Him in that Unity: however the All-Truth attains existence, it is through Himself.

That God is without cause

A necessary being has no cause whatsoever. Causes are of four kinds: that from which a thing has being, or the active cause; that on account of which a thing has being, or the final and completive cause; that in which a thing has being, or the material cause; and that through which a thing has being, or the formal cause.

The justification for limiting causes to these four varieties is that the reason for a thing is either internal in its subsistence, or a part of its being, or external to it. If it is internal, then it is either that part in which the thing is, potentially and not actually, that is to say its matter; or it is that part in which the thing becomes actually, that is to say its form. If it is external, then it can only be either that from which the thing has being, that is to say the agent, or that on account of which the thing has being, that is to say its purpose and end.

Since it is established that these are the roots and principles of this matter, let us rest on them and clarify the problems which are constructed upon them.

Demonstration that He has no active cause: This is self-evident: for if He had any reason for being, this would be adventitious and that would be a necessary being. Since it is established that He has no active cause, it follows on this line of reasoning that His Quiddity is not other than His Identity, that is to say, other than His Being; neither will He be a subsistence or an accident. There cannot be two, each of which derives its being from the other; nor can He be a necessary being in one respect, and a contingent being in another respect.

Proof that His Quiddity is not other than His Identity, but rather that His Being is unified in His Reality: If His Being were not the same as His Reality, then His Being would be other than His Reality. Every accident is caused, and every thing caused requires a reason. Now this reason is either external to His Quiddity, or is itself His Quiddity: if it is external, then He is not a necessary being, and is not exempt from an active cause; while if the reason is itself the Quiddity, then the reason must necessarily be itself a complete being in order that the being of another may result from it. Quiddity before being has no being; and if it had being before this, it would not require a second being. The question therefore returns to the problem of being. If the Being of the Quiddity is accidental, whence did this Being supervene and adhere? It is therefore established that the Identity of the Necessary Being is His Quiddity, and that He has no active cause; the necessary nature of His Being is like the quiddity of all other things. From this it is evident that the Necessary Being does not resemble any other thing in any respect whatsoever; for with all other things their being is other than their quiddity.

Proof that He is not an accident: An accident is a being in a locus. The locus is precedent to it, and its being is not possible without the locus. But we have stated that a being which is necessary has no reason for its being.

Proof that there cannot be two necessary beings, each deriving its being from the other: Each of them, in as much as it derives its being from the other, would be subsequent to the other, while at the same time by virtue of supplying being to the other, each would be precedent to the other: but one and the same thing cannot be both precedent and subsequent in relation to its being. Moreover, if we assume for the sake of argument that the other is non-existent: would the first then be a necessary being, or not? If it were a necessary being, it would have no connexion with the other: if it were not a necessary being, it would be a contingent being and would require another necessary being. Since the Necessary Being is One, and does not derive Its being from any one, it follows that He is a Necessary Being in every respect; while anything else derives its being from another.

Proof that He cannot be a Necessary Being in one respect and a contingent being in another respect: Such a being, in as much as it is a contingent being, would be connected in being with something else, and so it has a reason; but in as much as it is a necessary being, it would have no connexions with anything else. In that case it would both have being and not have being; and that is absurd.

Demonstration that He has no material and receptive cause: The receptive cause is the cause for the provision of the place in which a thing is received; that is to say, the place prepared for the reception of being, or the perfection of being. Now the Necessary Being is a perfection in pure actuality, and is not impaired by any deficiency; every perfection belongs to Him, derives from Him, and is preceded by His Essence, while every deficiency, even if it be metaphorical, is negated to Him. All perfection and all beauty are of His Being; indeed, these are the vestiges of the perfection of His Being; how then should He derive perfection from any other? Since it is thus established that He has no receptive cause, it follows that He does not possess anything potentially, and that He has no attribute yet to be awaited; on the contrary, His Perfection has been realized in actuality; and He has no material cause. We say "realized in actuality," using this as a common term of expression, meaning that every perfection belonging to any other is non-existent and yet to be awaited, whereas all perfection belonging to Him has being and is present. His Perfect Essence, preceding all relations, is One. From this it is manifest that His Attributes are not an augmentation of His Essence; for if they were an augmentation of His Essence, the Attributes would be potential with reference to the Essence and the Essence would be the reason for the Attributes. In that case the Attributes would be subsequent to a precedent, so that they would be in one respect active and in another receptive; their being active would be other than the aspect of their being receptive; and in consequence they would possess two mutually exclusive aspects. Now this is impossible in the case of anything whatsoever; when a body is in motion, the motivation is from one quarter and the movement from another.

If it were to be stated that His Attributes are not an augmentation of His Essence, but that they entered into the constitution of the Essence, and that the Essence cannot be conceived of as existing without these Attributes, then the Essence would be compound, and the Oneness would be destroyed. It is also evident, as a result of denying the existence of a receptive cause, that it is impossible for Him to change; for the meaning of change is the passing away of one attribute and the establishment of another; and if He were susceptible to change, He would possess potentially an element of passing-away and an element of establishment; and that is absurd. It is clear from this that He has no opposite and no contrary; for opposites are essences which succeed each other in the occupation of a single locus, there being between them the extreme of contrariety. But He is not receptive to accidents, much less to opposites. And if the term "opposite" is used to denote one who disputes with Him in His Rulership, it is clear too on this count that He has no opposite. It is further clear that it is impossible for Him not to be; for since it is established that His Being is necessary, it follows that it is impossible for Him not to be; because everything which exists potentially cannot exist actually, otherwise it would have two aspects. Anything which is receptive to a thing does not cease to be receptive when reception has actually taken place; if this were not so, it would result in the removal of both being and not-being, and that is untenable. This rule applies to every essence and every unified reality, such as angels and human spirits; they are not susceptible to not-being at all, since they are free from corporeal adjunctions.

Demonstration that He has no formal cause: A formal, corporeal cause only exists and is confirmed when a thing is possessed of matter: the matter has a share in the being of the form, in the same way that the form has a part in the disposition of the matter in being in actuality; such a thing is therefore caused. It is further evident as a result of denying this cause to Him, that He is also to be denied all corporeal attributes, such as time, space, direction, and being in one place to the exclusion of all other; in short, whatever is possible in relation to corporeal things is impossible in relation to Him.

Proof that He has no final cause: The final cause is that on account of which a thing has being; and the First Truth has not being for the sake of anything, rather does everything exist on account of the perfection of His Essence, being consequent to His Being and derived from His Being. Moreover the final cause, even if it be posterior in respect of being to all other causes, yet it is mentally prior to them all. It is the final cause which makes the active cause become a cause in actuality, that is to say in respect of its being a final cause.

Since it is established that He is exalted above this last kind of cause too, it is clear that there is no cause to His Attributes. It is also evident that He is Pure Benevolence and True Perfection; the meaning of His Self-Sufficiency likewise becomes manifest, namely that he approves of nothing and disapproves of nothing. For if He approved of anything, that thing would come into being and would continue to be; while if He disapproved of anything, that thing would be converted into not-being and would be annulled. The very divergency of these beings proves the nullity of such a proposition; for a thing which is one in every respect cannot approve of a thing and of its opposite. It is also not necessary for Him to observe the rule of greater expediency or of expediency, as certain Qualitarians have idly pretended; for if His acts of expediency were obligatory to Him, He would not merit gratitude and praise for such acts, since He would merely be fulfilling that which it is His obligation to perform, and He would be to all intents and purposes as one paying a debt; He would therefore deserve nothing at all for such benevolence. In fact His acts proceed on the contrary from Him and for Him. . . .

His attributes as interpreted according to the foregoing principles

Since it is established that God is a Necessary Being, that He is One in every respect, that He is exalted above all causes, and that He has no reason of any kind for His Being; since it is further established that His Attributes do not augment His Essence, and that He is qualified by the Attributes of Praise and Perfection; it follows necessarily that we must state that He is Knowing, Living, Willing, Omnipotent, Speaking, Seeing, Hearing, and Possessed of all the other Loveliest Attributes. It is also necessary to recognize that His Attributes are to be classified as negative, positive, and a compound of the two: since His Attributes are of this order, it follows that their multiplicity does not destroy His Unity or contradict the necessary nature of His Being. Pre-eternity for instance is essentially the negation of not-being in the first place, and the denial of causality and of primality in the second place; similarly the term One means that He is indivisible in every respect, both verbally and actually. When it is stated that He is a Necessary Being, this means that He is a Being without a cause, and that He is the Cause of other than Himself: this is a combination of the negative and the positive. Examples of the positive Attributes are His being Creator, Originator, Shaper, and the entire Attributes of Action. As for the compound of both, this kind is illustrated by His being Willing and Omnipotent, for these Attributes are a compound of Knowledge with the addition of Creativeness.

36. *Al-Ghazzali (1058–1111)*, Confessions

Reprinted by permission of the publisher from *The Confessions of Al Ghazzali,* trans. Claud Field, The Wisdom of the East Series (London: John Murray [Publishers] Ltd., 1908), pp. 25–30, 33–34.

Concerning the Philosophical Sects and the Stigma of Infidelity Which Attaches to Them All.

The philosophical systems, in spite of their number and variety, may be reduced to three (1) The Materialists; (2) The Naturalists; (3) The Theists.

(1) *The Materialists.* They reject an intelligent and omnipotent Creator and Disposer of the Universe. In their view the world exists from all eternity and had no author. The animal comes from semen and semen from the animal; so it has always been and will always be; those who maintain this doctrine are atheists.

(2) *The Naturalists.* These devote themselves to the study of nature and of the marvellous phenomena of the animal and vegetable world. Having carefully analysed animal organs with the help of anatomy, struck with the wonders of God's work and with the wisdom therein revealed, they are forced to admit the existence of a wise Creator Who knows the end and purpose of everything. And certainly no one can

study anatomy and the wonderful mechanism of living things without being obliged to confess the profound wisdom of Him Who has framed the bodies of animals and especially of man. But carried away by their natural researches they believed that the existence of a being absolutely depended upon the proper equilibrium of its organism. According to them, as the latter perishes and is destroyed, so is the thinking faculty which is bound up with it; and as they assert that the restoration of a thing once destroyed to existence is unthinkable, they deny the immortality of the soul. Consequently they deny heaven, hell, resurrection, and judgment. Acknowledging neither a recompense for good deeds nor a punishment for evil ones, they fling off all authority and plunge into sensual pleasures with the avidity of brutes. These also ought to be called atheists, for the true faith depends not only on the acknowledgment of God, but of His Apostle and of the Day of Judgment. And although they acknowledge God and His attributes, they deny a judgment to come.

(3) Next come the *Theists.* Among them should be reckoned Socrates, who was the teacher of Plato as Plato was of Aristotle. This latter drew up for his disciples the rules of logic, organised the sciences, elucidated what was formerly obscure, and expounded what had not been understood. This school refuted the systems of the two others, i.e. the Materialists and Naturalists; but in exposing their mistaken and perverse beliefs, they made use of arguments which they should not. "God suffices to protect the faithful in war" (*Koran,* xxxiii. 25).

Aristotle also contended with success against the theories of Plato, Socrates, and the theists who had preceded him, and separated himself entirely from them; but he could not eliminate from his doctrine the stains of infidelity and heresy which disfigure the teaching of his predecessors. We should therefore consider them all as unbelievers, as well as the so-called Mussulman philosophers, such as Ibn Sina [Avicenna] and Farabi, who have adopted their systems.

Let us, however, acknowledge that among Mussulman philosophers none have better interpreted the doctrine of Aristotle than the latter. What others have handed down as his teaching is full of error, confusion, and obscurity adapted to disconcert the reader. The unintelligible can neither be accepted nor rejected. The philosophy of Aristotle, all serious knowledge of which we owe to the translation of these two learned men, may be divided into three portions: the first contains matter justly chargeable with impiety, the second is tainted with heresy, and the third we are obliged to reject absolutely. We proceed to details:

DIVISIONS OF THE PHILOSOPHIC SCIENCES.

These sciences, in relation to the aim we have set before us, may be divided into six sections: (1) Mathematics; (2) Logic; (3) Physics; (4) Metaphysics; (5) Politics; (6) Moral Philosophy.

Mathematics comprises the knowledge of calculation, geometry, and cosmography: it has no connection with the religious sciences, and proves nothing for or against religion; it rests on a foundation of proofs which, once known and understood, cannot be refuted. Mathematics tend, however, to produce two bad results.

The first is this: Whoever studies this science admires the subtlety and clearness of its proofs. His confidence in philosophy increases, and he thinks that all its departments are capable of the same clearness and solidity of proof as mathematics. But when he hears people speak of the unbelief and impiety of mathematicians, of their professed disregard for the Divine Law, which is notorious, it is true that, out of regard for authority, he echoes these accusations, but he says to himself at the same time that, if there was truth in religion, it would not have escaped those who have displayed so much keenness of intellect in the study of mathematics.

Next, when he becomes aware of the unbelief and rejection of religion on the part of these learned men, he concludes that to reject religion is reasonable. How many of such men gone astray I have met whose sole argument was that just mentioned. And supposing one puts to them the following objection: "It does not follow that a man who excels in one branch of knowledge excels in all others, nor that he should be equally versed in jurisprudence, theology, and medicine. It is possible to be entirely ignorant of metaphysics, and yet to be an excellent grammarian. There are past masters in every science who are entirely ignorant of other branches of knowledge. The arguments of the ancient philosophers are rigidly demonstrative in mathematics and only conjectural in religious questions. In order to ascertain this one must proceed to a thorough examination of the matter." Supposing, I say, one makes the above objection to these "apes of unbelief," they find it distasteful. Falling a prey to their passions, to a besotted vanity, and the wish to pass for learned men, they persist in maintaining the pre-eminence of mathematicians in all branches of knowledge. This is a serious evil, and for this reason those who study mathematics should be checked from going too far in their researches. For though far removed as it may be from the things of religion, this study, serving as it does as an introduction to the philosophic systems, casts over religion its malign influence. It is rarely that a man devotes himself to it without robbing himself of his faith and casting off the restraints of religion.

The second evil comes from the sincere but ignorant Mussulman who thinks the best way to defend religion is by rejecting all the exact sciences. Accusing their professors of being astray, he rejects their theories of the eclipses of the sun and moon, and condemns them in the name of religion. These accusations are carried far and wide, they reach the ears of the philosopher who knows that these theories rest on infallible proofs; far from losing confidence in them, he believes, on the contrary, that Islam has ignorance and the denial of scientific proofs for its basis, and his devotion to philosophy increases with his hatred to religion.

It is therefore a great injury to religion to suppose that the defence of Islam involves the condemnation of the exact sciences. The religious law contains nothing which approves them or condemns them, and in their turn they make no attack on religion. The words of the Prophet, "The sun and the moon are two signs of the power of God; they are not eclipsed for the birth or the death of any one; when you see these signs take refuge in prayer and invoke the name of God"—these words, I say, do not in any way condemn the astronomical calculations which define the orbits of these two bodies, their conjunction and opposition according to particular laws. But as for the so-called tradition, "When God reveals Himself in anything, He abases Himself thereto," it is unauthentic, and not found in any trustworthy collection of the traditions.

Such is the bearing and the possible danger of mathematics. . . .

Metaphysics. This is the fruitful breeding-ground of the errors of philosophers. Here they can no longer satisfy the laws of rigorous argumentation such as logic demands, and this is what explains the disputes which arise between them in the study of metaphysics. The system most closely akin to the system of the Muhammedan doctors is that of Aristotle as expounded to us by Farabi and Avicenna. The sum total of their errors can be reduced to twenty propositions: three of them are irreligious, and the other seventeen heretical. It was in order to combat their system that we wrote the work *Destruction of the Philosophers.* The three propositions in which they are opposed to all the doctrines of Islam are the following:

(1) Bodies do not rise again; spirits alone will be rewarded or punished; future punishments will be therefore spiritual and not physical. They are right in admitting spiritual punishments, for there will be such; but they are wrong in rejecting physical punishments, and contradicting in this manner the assertions of the Divine Law.

(2) "God takes cognisance of universals, not of specials." This is manifestly irreligious. The Koran asserts truly, "Not an atom's weight in heaven or earth can escape His knowledge" (x. 62).

(3) They maintain that the universe exists from all eternity and will never end.

None of these propositions have ever been admitted by Moslems.

Besides this, they deny that God has attributes, and maintain that He knows by His essence only and not by means of any attribute accessory to His essence. In this point they approach the doctrine of the Mutazilites, doctrines which we are not obliged to condemn as irreligious. On the contrary, in our work entitled *Criteria of the differences which divide Islam from Atheism,* we have proved the wrongness of those who accuse of irreligion everything which is opposed to their way of looking at things.

37. *Ibn Khaldun (1332–1406)*, Muqaddimah

Bedouins Are Prior to Sedentary People. The Desert Is the Basis and Reservoir of Civilization and Cities.

We have mentioned that the Bedouins restrict themselves to the [bare] necessities in their conditions [of life] and are unable to go beyond them, while sedentary people concern themselves with conveniences and luxuries in their conditions and customs. The [bare] necessities are no doubt prior to the conveniences and luxuries. [Bare] necessities, in a way, are basic, and luxuries secondary and an outgrowth [of the necessities]. Bedouins, thus, are the basis of, and prior to, cities and sedentary people. Man seeks first the [bare] necessities. Only after he has obtained the [bare] necessities, does he get to comforts and luxuries. The toughness of desert life precedes the softness of sedentary life. Therefore, urbanization is found to be the goal of the Bedouin. He aspires to [that goal]. Through his own efforts, he achieves what he proposes to achieve in this respect. When he has obtained enough to be ready for the conditions and customs of luxury, he enters upon a life of ease and submits himself to the yoke of the city. This is the case with all Bedouin tribes. Sedentary people, on the other hand, have no desire for desert conditions, unless they are motivated by some urgent necessity or they cannot keep up with their fellow city dwellers.

Evidence for the fact that Bedouins are the basis of, and prior to, sedentary people is furnished by investigating the inhabitants of any given city. We shall find that most of its inhabitants originated among Bedouins dwelling in the country and villages of the vicinity. Such Bedouins became wealthy, settled in the city, and adopted a life of ease and luxury, such as exists in the sedentary environment. This proves that sedentary conditions are secondary to desert conditions and that they are the basis of them. This should be understood.

All Bedouins and sedentary people differ also among themselves in their conditions [of life]. Many a clan is greater than another, many a tribe greater than another, many a city larger than another, and many a town more populous [*ʿumrân*] than another.

It has thus become clear that the existence of Bedouins is prior to, and the basis of, the existence of towns and cities. Likewise, the existence of towns and cities results from luxury customs pertaining to luxury and ease, which are posterior to the customs that go with the bare necessities of life. . . .

Only Tribes Held Together by Group Feeling Can Live in the Desert.

It should be known that God put good and evil into the nature of man. Thus, He said in the Qur'ân: "We led him along the two paths." He further said: "And inspired [the soul] with its wickedness as well as its fear of God."

Evil is the quality that is closest to man when he fails to improve his customs and [when] religion is not used as the model to improve him. The great mass of mankind is in that condition, with the exception of those to whom God gives success. Evil qualities in man are injustice and mutual aggression. He who casts his eye upon the property of his brother will lay his hand upon it to take it, unless there is a restraining influence to hold him back. The poet thus said:

> Injustice is a human characteristic. If you find
> A moral man, there is some reason why he is not unjust.

Mutual aggression of people in towns and cities is averted by the authorities and the government, which hold back the masses under their control from attacks and aggression upon each other. They are thus prevented by the influence of force and governmental authority from mutual injustice, save such injustice as comes from the ruler himself.

Aggression against a city from outside may be averted by walls, in the event of negligence, a surprise attack at night, or inability [of the inhabitants] to withstand the enemy during the day. [Or,] it may be averted with the help of a militia of government auxiliary troops, if [the inhabitants are otherwise] prepared and ready to offer resistance.

The restraining influence among Bedouin tribes comes from their *shaykhs* and leaders. It results from the great respect and veneration they generally enjoy among the people. The hamlets of the Bedouins are defended against outside enemies by a tribal militia composed of noble youths of the tribe who are known for their courage. Their defense and protection are successful only if they are a closely-knit group of common descent. This strengthens their stamina and makes them feared, since everybody's affection for his family and his group is more important [than anything else]. Compassion and affection for one's blood relations and relatives exist in human nature as something God put into the hearts of men. It makes for mutual support and aid, and increases the fear felt by the enemy.

This may be exemplified by the story in the Qur'ân about Joseph's brothers. They said to their father: "If the wolf eats him, while we are a group, then, indeed, we have lost out." This means that one cannot imagine any hostile act being undertaken against anyone who has his group feeling to support him.

Those who have no one of their own lineage [to care for] rarely feel affection for their fellows. If danger is in the air on the day of battle, such a one slinks away and seeks to save himself, because he is afraid of being left without support and dreads [that prospect]. Such people, therefore, cannot live in the desert, because they would fall prey to any nation that might want to swallow them up.

If this is true with regard to the place where one lives, which is in constant need of defense and military protection, it is equally true with regard to every other human activity, such as prophecy, the establishment of royal authority, or propaganda [for a cause]. Nothing can be achieved in these matters without fighting for it, since man has the natural urge to offer resistance. And for fighting one cannot do without group feeling, as we mentioned at the beginning. This should be taken as the guiding principle of our later exposition.

God gives success.

Group Feeling Results Only from [Blood] Relationship or Something Corresponding to It.

[Respect for] blood ties is something natural among men, with the rarest exceptions. It leads to affection for one's relations and blood relatives, [the feeling that] no harm ought to befall them nor any destruction come upon them. One feels shame when one's relatives are treated unjustly or attacked, and one wishes to intervene between them and whatever peril or destruction threatens them. This is a natural urge in man, for as long as there have been human beings. If the direct relationship between persons who help each other is very close, so that it leads to close contact and unity, the ties are obvious and clearly require the [existence of a feeling of solidarity] without any outside [prodding]. If, however, the relationship is somewhat distant, it is often forgotten in part. However, some knowledge of it remains and this causes a person to help his relatives for the known motive, in order to escape the shame he would feel in his soul were a person to whom he is somehow related treated unjustly.

Clients and allies belong in the same category. The affection everybody has for his clients and allies results from the feeling of shame that comes to a person when one of his neighbors, relatives, or a blood relation in any degree [of kinship] is humiliated. The reason for it is that a client[-master] relationship leads to close contact exactly, or approximately in the same way, as does common descent. It is in that sense that one must understand Muḥammad's remark, "Learn as much of your pedigrees as is necessary to establish your ties of blood relationship." It means that pedigrees are useful only in so far as they imply the close contact that is a consequence of blood ties and that eventually leads to mutual help and affection. Anything beyond that is superfluous. For a pedigree is something imaginary and devoid of reality. Its usefulness consists only in the resulting connection and close contact. If the fact of [common descent] is obvious and clear, it evokes in man a natural affection, as we have said. If, however, its existence is known only from remote history, it moves the imagination but faintly. Its usefulness is gone, and preoccupation with it becomes gratuitous, a kind of game, and as such is not permissible. In this sense, one must understand the remark, "Genealogy is something that is of no use to know and that it does no harm not to know." This means that when common descent is no longer clear and has become a matter of scientific knowledge, it can no longer move the imagination and is denied the affection caused by group feeling. It has become useless.

And God knows better. . . .

The Goal to Which Group Feeling Leads Is Royal Authority.

This is because, as we have mentioned before, group feeling gives protection and makes possible mutual defense, the pressing of claims, and every other kind of social activity. We have also mentioned before that according to their nature, human beings need someone to act as a restraining influence and mediator in every social organization, in order to keep the members from [fighting] with each other. That person must, by necessity, have superiority over the others in the matter of group feeling. If not, his power to [exercise a restraining influence] could not materialize. Such superiority is royal authority [*mulk*]. It is more than leadership. Leadership means being a chieftain, and the leader is obeyed, but he has no power to force others to accept his rulings. Royal authority means superiority and the power to rule by force.

When a person sharing in the group feeling has reached the rank of chieftain and commands obedience, and when he then finds the way open toward superiority and [the use of] force, he follows that way, because it is something desirable. He cannot completely achieve his [goal] except with the help of the group feeling, which causes [the others] to obey him. Thus, royal superiority is a goal to which group feeling leads, as one can see.

Even if an individual tribe has different "houses" and many diverse group feelings, still, there must exist a group feeling that is stronger than all the other group feelings combined, that is superior to them all and makes them subservient, and in which all the diverse group feelings coalesce, as it were, to become one greater group feeling. Otherwise, splits would occur and lead to dissension and strife. "If God did not keep human beings apart, the earth would perish."

Once group feeling has established superiority over the people who share [in that particular group feeling], it will, by its very nature, seek superiority over people of other group feelings unrelated to the first. If the one [group feeling] is the equal of the other or is able to stave off [its challenge], the [competing people] are even with and equal to each other. [In this case,] each group feeling maintains its sway over its own domain and people, as is the case with tribes and nations all over the earth. However, if the one group feeling overpowers the other and makes it subservient to itself, the two group feelings enter into close contact, and the [defeated] group feeling gives added power to the [victorious] group feeling, which, as a result, sets its goal of superiority and domination higher than before. In this way, it goes on until the power of that particular group feeling equals the power of the ruling dynasty. Then, when the ruling dynasty grows senile and no defender arises from among its friends who share in its group feeling, the [new group feeling] takes over and deprives the ruling dynasty of its power, and, thus, obtains complete royal authority.

The power of [a given group feeling] may [also] reach its peak when the ruling dynasty has not yet reached senility. [This stage] may coincide with the stage at which [the ruling dynasty] needs to have recourse to the people who represent the various group feelings [in order to master the situation]. In such a case, the ruling dynasty incorporates [the people who enjoy the powerful group feeling] among its clients whom it uses for the execution of its various projects. This, then, means [the formation of] another royal authority, inferior to that of the controlling royal authority. This was the case with the Turks under the ʿAbbâsids, with the Ṣinhâjah and the Zanâtah in their relation to the Kutâmah, and with the Ḥamdânids in their relation to the [Fâṭimid] ʿAlids and the ʿAbbâsids.

It is thus evident that royal authority is the goal of group feeling. When [group feeling] attains that goal, the tribe [representing that particular group feeling] obtains royal authority, either by seizing actual control or by giving assistance [to the ruling dynasty]. It depends on the circumstances prevailing at a given time [which of the two alternatives applies]. If the group feeling encounters obstacles on its way to the goal, as we shall explain, it stops where it is, until God decides what is going to happen to it.

Obstacles on the Way Toward Royal Authority Are Luxury and the Submergence of the Tribe in a Life of Prosperity.

The reason for this is that, when a tribe has achieved a certain measure of superiority with the help of its group feeling, it gains control over a corresponding amount of wealth and comes to share prosperity and abundance with those who have been in possession of these things [for a long time]. It shares in them to the degree of its power and usefulness to the ruling dynasty. If the ruling dynasty is so strong that no one would think of depriving it of its power or sharing [its power] with it, the tribe in question submits to its rule and is satisfied with whatever share in the dynasty's wealth and tax revenue it is permitted to enjoy. Hopes would not go so high as to [think of] the royal prerogatives or ways to obtain the [royal authority. Members of the tribe] are merely concerned with prosperity, gain, and a life of abundance. [They are satisfied] to lead an easy, restful life in the shadow of the ruling dynasty, and to adopt royal habits in building and dress, a matter they stress and in which they take more and more pride, the more luxuries and plenty they obtain, as well as all the other things that go with luxury and plenty.

As a result, the toughness of desert life is lost. Group feeling and courage weaken. Members of the tribe revel in the well-being that God has given them. Their children and offspring grow up too proud to look after themselves or to attend to their own needs. They have disdain also for all the other things that are necessary in connection with group feeling. This finally becomes a character trait and natural characteristic of theirs. Their group feeling and courage decrease in the next generations. Eventually, group feeling is altogether destroyed. They thus invite [their] own destruction. The greater their luxury and the easier the life they enjoy, the closer they are to extinction, not to mention [their lost chance of obtaining] royal authority. The things that go with luxury and submergence in a life of ease break the vigor of the group feeling, which alone produces superiority. When group feeling is destroyed, the tribe is no longer able to defend or protect itself, let alone press any claims. It will be swallowed up by other nations.

It has thus become clear that luxury is an obstacle on the way toward royal authority. "God gives His kingdom [royal authority] to whomever He wants to give it." . . .

The Transition of Dynasties from Desert Life to Sedentary Culture.

It should be known that these stages are natural ones for dynasties. The superiority through which royal authority is achieved is the result of group feeling and of the great energy and rapacious habits which go with it. As a rule, these things are possible only in connection with desert life. The first stage of dynasties, therefore, is that of desert life.

When royal authority is obtained, it is accompanied by a life of ease and increased opportunities. Sedentary culture is merely a diversification of luxury and a refined knowledge of the crafts employed for the diverse aspects and ways of [luxury]. This concerns, for instance, food, clothing, building, bedding [carpets], utensils, and other household needs. Each one of these things requires special interdependent crafts serving to refine and improve it. [These crafts] increase in number with the [growing] variety of pleasures and amusements and ways and means to enjoy the life of luxury the soul desires, and [with the growing number of] different things to which people get used.

The sedentary stage of royal authority follows the stage of desert life. It does so of necessity, as a result of the fact that royal authority is of necessity accompanied by a life of ease. In the sedentary stage and under [sedentary] conditions, the people of a given dynasty always follow the traditions of the preceding dynasty. They observe with their own eyes the circumstances [under which the preceding dynasty lived], and, as a rule, learn from them.

Something of the sort happened to the Arabs during the conquest by which they came to rule the Persians and Byzantines and made their daughters and sons their servants. At that time, the Arabs had no sedentary culture at all. The story goes that when they were given a pillow they supposed it was a bundle of rags. The camphor they found in the treasuries of the Persian king was used by them as salt in their dough. There are many similar things. The Arabs, then, enslaved the people of the former dynasties and employed them in their occupations and their household needs. From among them, they selected skilled masters of the various [crafts], and were in turn taught by them to handle, master, and develop them for themselves. In addition, the circumstances of the Arabs' life widened and became more diversified. Thus, they reached the limit in this respect. They entered the stage of sedentary culture, of luxury and refinement in food, drink, clothing, building, weapons, bedding [carpets], household goods, music, and all other commodities and furnishings. The same [perfection they showed] on their gala days, banquets, and wedding nights. In this respect, they surpassed the limit. . . .

The Stages of Dynasties. How the Desert Attitude Differs Among the People in the Different Stages.

It should be known that a dynasty goes through different stages and encounters new conditions. Through the conditions that are peculiar to a particular stage, the supporters of the dynasty acquire in that stage traits of character such as do not exist in any other stage. Traits of character are the natural result of the peculiar situations in which they are found.

The conditions and stages of a dynasty are as a rule no more than five [in number].

The first stage is that of success, the overthrow of all opposition, and the appropriation of royal authority from the preceding dynasty. In this stage, the ruler serves as model to his people by the manner in which he acquires glory, collects taxes, defends property, and provides military protection. He does not claim anything exclusively for himself to the exclusion of [his people], because [such an attitude] is what is required by group feeling, [and it was group feeling] that gave superiority [to the dynasty], and [group feeling] still continues to exist as before.

The second stage is the one in which the ruler gains complete control over his people, claims royal authority all for himself, excluding them, and prevents them from trying to have a share in it. In this stage, the ruler of the dynasty is concerned with gaining adherents and acquiring clients and followers in great numbers, so as to be able to blunt the aspirations of the people who share in his group feeling and belong to his group, who are of the same descent as he himself and have the same claim to royal authority as he has. He keeps them from power and bars them from the sources of [power]. He stops them from getting to it, and, eventually, all the power is in the hands of his family. He reserves all the glory that he is building up to the members of his own house. He spends as much, or more, care to keep [his people] at a distance and to subdue them, as the first members of the dynasty expended in the search for power. The first [members of the dynasty] kept strangers away, and all the people who shared in their group feeling supported them in this. He, on the other hand, keeps [his] relatives away, and he is supported in this effort only by a very small number of people, who are not related to him. Thus, he undertakes a very difficult task.

The third stage is one of leisure and tranquillity in which the fruits of royal authority are enjoyed. [These fruits are] the things that human nature desires, such as acquisition of property, creation of lasting monuments, and fame. All the ability [of the ruler] is expended on collecting taxes; regulating income and expenses, bookkeeping and planning expenditures; erecting large buildings, big constructions, spacious cities, and lofty monuments; presenting gifts to embassies of nobles from [foreign] nations and tribal dignitaries; and dispensing bounty to his own people. In addition, he supports the demands of his followers and retinue with money and positions. He inspects his soldiers, pays them well, and distributes fairly their allowances every month. Eventually, the result of this [liberality] shows itself in their dress, their fine equipment, and their armor on parade days. The ruler thus can impress friendly dynasties and frighten hostile ones with [his soldiers]. This stage is the last during which the ruler is in complete authority. Throughout this and the previous stages, the rulers are independent in their opinions. They build up their strength and show the way for those after them.

The fourth stage is one of contentment and peacefulness. The ruler is content with what his predecessors have built. He lives in peace with all his royal peers. He adopts the tradition of his predecessors and follows closely in their footsteps. He imitates their ways most carefully. He thinks that to depart from tradition would mean the destruction of his power and that they knew better [what is good for the preservation of] the glory they themselves had built.

The fifth stage is one of waste and squandering. In this stage, the ruler wastes on pleasures and amusements [the treasures] accumulated by his ancestors, through [excessive] generosity to his inner circle and at their parties. Also, he acquires bad, low-class followers to whom he entrusts the most important matters [of state], which they are not qualified to handle by themselves, not knowing which of them they should tackle and which they should leave alone. [In addition,] the ruler seeks to destroy the great clients of his people and followers of his predecessors. Thus, they come to hate him and conspire to refuse support to him. [Furthermore] he loses a number of soldiers by spending their allowances on his pleasures [instead of paying them] and by refusing them access to his person and not supervising them [properly]. Thus, he ruins the foundations his ancestors had laid and tears down what they had built up. In this stage, the dynasty is seized by senility and the chronic disease from which it can hardly ever rid itself, for which it can find no cure, and, eventually, it is destroyed. We shall explain that in connection with conditions to be discussed later on.

God is the best heir. . . .

How a New Dynasty Originates.

It should be known that when the ruling dynasty starts on the road to senility and destruction, the rise and beginning of the new dynasty takes place in two ways:

[The one way is] for provincial governors in the dynasty to gain control over remote regions when [the dynasty] loses its influence there. Each one of them founds a new dynasty for his people and a realm to be perpetuated in his family. His children or clients inherit it from him. Gradually, they have a flourishing realm. They often compete bitterly with each other and aspire to gain sole possession of it. The one who is stronger than his rival will gain the upper hand and take away what the other had.

This happened in the ʿAbbâsid dynasty when it started on the road to senility and its shadow receded from the remote regions. The Sâmânids gained control over Transoxania, the Ḥamdânids over Mosul and Syria, and the Ṭûlûnids over Egypt. The same thing happened in the Umayyad dynasty in Spain. Their realm was divided among the *reyes de taïfas* who had been their provincial governors. It was divided into several dynasties with several rulers, who passed their realms on after their death to their relatives or clients. This way of forming a new dynasty avoids the possibility of war between the [new rulers] and the ruling dynasty. [These new rulers] are already firmly established in their leadership and do not want to gain domination over the ruling dynasty. The latter is affected by senility, and its shadow recedes from the remote regions of the realm and can no [longer] reach them.

The other way is for some rebel from among the neighboring nations and tribes to revolt against the dynasty. He either makes propaganda for some particular cause to which he intends to win the people, as we have indicated, or he possesses great power and a great group feeling among his people. His power is already flourishing among them, and now he aspires with the help of [his people] to gain royal authority. [His people] are convinced that they will obtain it, because they feel that they are superior to the ruling dynasty, which is affected by senility. Thus, to [the rebel] and his people, it is a fact that they will gain domination over it. They constantly attack it, until they defeat it and inherit its power.

This was the case with the Saljûqs in relation to the descendants of Sebuktigîn, and with the Merinids in the Maghrib in relation to the Almohads.

"God has the power to execute His commands."